Defy Mediocrity

<u>The</u> Employee's 90 Minute Guide To Excellence

D1496173

Derrick W. Welch

LeeMar Publishing
319 Centre Ave
Suite 178
Rockland, MA 02370

Other books by the author:

In Pursuit of Profits: How To At Least Double Your Profits Without Increasing Your Sales

ISBN ---1886262-01-2

Today we live in a suit happy society in which no one takes responsibility for anything. Between lawyers and the government, business has less and less control each year and more and more liability. Like it or not, and I don't, this is the world we live in. Therefore, I must add the following disclaimer:

This publication contains the opinions and ideas of its author and is designed to provide useful advice in regard to the subject matter covered. It is sold with the understanding that the author and publisher are not engaged in rendering legal, accounting or other professional services. The author and publisher specifically disclaim any responsibility for any liability, loss or risk, personal or otherwise, which is incurred as a consequence, directly or indirectly, of the use and the application of any of the contents of this book. If these terms are not agreeable to you please return this book to the publisher for a full refund within 30 days of purchase.

With that said, I will also point out that I will claim no credit for any success you enjoy as a result of reading and implementing my ideas. After all, fair is fair.

Cover Design by Katherine Conley

Dedication

To my mother and father. They are, and have always been, a never-ending source of inspiration, pride, and encouragement.

And

To Ginger. She took a piece of my heart with her when she went to the other side of the rainbow.

Acknowledgments

I wish to thank my wonderful wife Dianne, who has always been a source of support and encouragement to me, and my two daughters, who are my pride and joy, Jessica and Joanna. Without their constant support this book would never have been written.

I would also like to publicly thank John Nazzaro. A man who taught me much about what I could and could not do. A man who taught me how to expand my mind and how perception and reality are so different and yet the same. A man who had belief in me when I had doubt. A man who saw potential in me when I saw limitations. Thank you for your vision.

Table of Contents

Defy Mediocrity: <u>The</u> Employee's 90 Minute Guide To Excellence

A message from the author

"Those who defy mediocrity do not do extraordinary things. They do ordinary things extraordinarily well."

The difference between the employees who excel at their job and those who just get by lies in how they do their job. The difference between those who are considered valuable employees, the employees who move up more rapidly than others within the company, and those who are simply part of the staff lies not in major things, but in many minor things. The difference that will set you apart from others, from mediocrity, will come from many small things not a few major things.

<u>If you are seeking ways to make your job more secure in this age of employment instability, this book will show you how.</u> If you want to improve your on-the-job performance this book will show you how. If you want to develop your skills and value to the company, this book will show you how. If you want to become much better at what you do and how you do it, this book will show you how. <u>If you want to move ahead in your career as rapidly as possible, this book will show you how.</u>

Rising from mediocrity to excellence simply is not that difficult. The difference between an extraordinary employee and an ordinary one really is that little "extra". The little extra that spells the defeat of mediocrity.

This is a book about defying mediocrity. Defying mediocrity in the workplace, specifically. It is a book about overcoming the attitude of entitlement. It is a book about conquering complacency, apathy, procrastination, and dozens of other self-defeating traits so many of us have that hold us back in our careers and stop us from doing all we are capable of doing and of becoming. **This is a book about the pursuit of individual excellence!**

It is a book about making the most out of what you have. It is about producing results instead of creating excuses. This book will show you how to rise above mediocrity.

Few things in life cannot be overcome with the right combination of attitude and commitment. Mediocrity is one of the easiest things to defy.

It simply is not that hard to rise above the rest. It is simply not that hard to dramatically improve your on-the-job performance. It is simply not that hard to become far more valuable and capable. In fact, I think it takes more effort, and drains you more emotionally, to embrace mediocrity than it does to pursue excellence.

The quest for excellence, the quest to be the best you can at what you do, is a thrilling and evolutionary quest that will produce astounding results in every area of your life. If you think I am overstating this think about this.

The majority of your life revolves around your job. Yes, your job provides you the income you need to live. But think of how much time you spend on the job, going to the job, coming home from the job, talking about work, thinking about work, planning for work, and preparing for work. More than half of your waking life somehow revolves around what you do for a living, where you do it, and how well you do it.

Don't you think an attitude of complacency, apathy, doing enough to just get by, procrastination, and entitlement will carry over into other areas of your life? You see mediocrity manifests itself in many ways and cannot simply be turned on and off. **It is a silent killer of careers and dreams.**

On the other hand, the pursuit of improvement, the pursuit of excellence on the job, will also carry over to all other areas of your life. It simply is not possible to dramatically improve your job related activities and not see major improvements in your overall life.

Once you take the simple steps required to defeat mediocrity your attitude, commitment, and quest for constant improvement will carry over to every area of your life. It really is this simple!

Let me also point out what this book is not about. It is not about the power of positive thinking. It is not about loving yourself and loving others. It is not about "I'm O.K. You're O.K.". It is not about self-visualization. It is not about corporate politics and how to play the game to get ahead. It is not about transcendental meditation.

It is not about processes. It is not about reengineering your career. It is not about paradigms. It contains no academic idealism. I will leave this type of motivational writing to others.

<u>It is a blunt, hard hitting, no nonsense guide written to show you how to dramatically improve what you do and how you do it. It is about reality. The reality of rapidly moving ahead in your career.</u>

I will be aggressive with you at times. I will tell you things that you might not like to hear. I would not be doing you any great favors by sugar coating anything for you, so I won't.

It is about the things you can do to become far better at what you do and how you do it. It is about tapping into that tremendous potential you have. **It is about removing the road blocks that you have put in front of you. The road blocks that are holding you back from obtaining the on-the-job excellence you can so easily achieve**.

It is my hope that you will use these ideas and strategies to make the most of your talents and capabilities so that you can accomplish what you are truly capable of in your professional life. If I can play some small part in helping you achieve your goals, my efforts will be well rewarded.

My best,

Derrick W. Welch

Derrick W. Welch

Defy Mediocrity: <u>The</u> Employee's 90 Minute Guide To Excellence

Preface

Let me tell you a story. A story about the defiance of mediocrity. A story about someone who suffered setbacks, including many self-inflicted setbacks, and kept moving forward. A story about someone who never kidded himself about being better, smarter, or more capable than anyone else, but who always tried to make the most of what he had.

A story about a little boy who found out he could not walk like the other little boys and girls due to a serious hip problem. A little boy who spent more time in the hospital then he did at home. A little boy who went to first grade wearing a full leg brace on his right leg and a shoe on his left foot with a six inch lift. A little boy who walked to school that first day, and every day for 3 years, with his brace, his Herman Munster shoe, and the aid of crutches.

A little boy who could not play with his classmates at recess. A little boy who could only watch and could never join in. A little boy who had to ask others to get his lunch for him since he could not navigate the stairs to the lunch room to get his own lunch. A little boy who ate in the classroom alone each day.

A little boy who was so happy the day he was able to walk without his crutches and shoe and leg brace that he could never describe the feeling to others. A little boy who thought his ordeal was over the day they came off.

A little boy who grew into a young man. A young man who was cut from the sports teams he so longed to play for because his leg strength was never fully normal. A young man who once again had to watch from the sidelines. A young man who watched his brothers become fine athletes while he became the best booster he could.

A young man who began to walk with a limp in Jr. High School. A young man who was told that the leg with the hip problem was growing much slower than his normal leg and that this was what was causing his limp. A limp that would only get much worse if something wasn't done.

Derrick W. Welch

A young man who missed the entire eighth grade as he underwent surgery to correct the problem. Surgery that slowed down the growth of one leg so the other could catch up.

A young man who spent six months in a toe to hip cast. A young man who stayed home with a tutor every day. A young man who watched at the window each day as his friends romped in the front yard. A young man who rarely complained as he always understood so many others had much worse problems than he.

A young man who was never good enough to make the high school basketball, football, or baseball teams. A young man who was determined to overcome these problems and earn his high school letter in track. A young man who knew he would never have the leg strength he needed for these other sports but who did have the arm strength to throw a discus, javelin, and shotput. A young man who bought his own javelin with money he earned delivering papers and who spent hours alone in a nearby field learning how to throw that spear. A young man who refused to be left out and found a way to earn his letter.

A young man who was so stubborn that he moved out of his house as a teenager and went to live with a poor broken family in another part of town. A young man whose new roommate turned out to be a heroin addict.

A young man who had average grades in school but went on to college anyway. A young man who did little better in college. A man who left college after two years, got married, and at the age of 22, had a little girl. A man who was determined to finish what he had started and went back to college at night.

A man who once again stopped his studies a few years later as he had another little girl and was now working two jobs to support his family. A man who was later given the opportunity to join a major Boston-based advertising agency despite his lack of experience and education.

A man who, at the age of 27, was promoted at the agency to an account executive assigned to the agency's largest account. A $4 billion dollar bank. A man who was terrified of speaking in front of people.

A man who found that the job of account executive involved a great deal of public speaking, new business solicitation, and boardroom presentations.

A man who, when he gave his first formal presentation in front of a room full of executives, broke out into such a cold sweat he began to see stars and nearly passed out. Needless to say, the agency did not get this account. A man who dedicated himself to overcoming this fear and went on to win many new accounts, awards, and excellent reviews.

A man who was given the opportunity to take over all operations of a mutli-million dollar company at the age of 31, still without that college degree and without the experience to handle the job.

A man who went back to school 18 years later and finished the degree he had started so many years ago. In fact, he earned three degrees.

A man who overcame numerous minor obstacles, who pushed a never-ending source of excuses aside, who made the most of every opportunity he was given, and who always understood his limitations and problems were nothing compared to so many others. A man who was determined to defy mediocrity and learned how. A man who learned it simply isn't that hard to rise above the masses. To rise above mediocrity.

I know. I was that little boy. I will show you how.

Derrick W. Welch

Derrick W. Welch

Chapter 1. Mediocrity. What is it?

"Excellence is to do a common thing in an uncommon way."

Booker T. Washington

Webster's New Collegiate Dictionary defines mediocrity as follows: "the quality or state of being mediocre, moderate ability or value, a mediocre person". Webster's defines mediocre as "moderate or low quality". <u>Do these definitions describe you?</u> Low quality? Moderate ability? Do they describe the people you work with? Do they describe the effort put forth by you or those you interact with each day? Is this how you feel about yourself? Your on-the-job performance? Is this how others in the company see you or would describe you?

Now I understand the good folks at Webster's are describing the term mediocrity in a very general sense, but I want to discuss it specifically. Very specifically. I want to discuss it as it pertains to the workplace. I want to discuss it as it pertains to your efforts and the efforts of those you interact with.

Speaking as an employer, an employee, co-worker, and customer, I can say without hesitation that mediocrity surrounds us. It has become an epidemic. It is a disease that is destroying the ability of every company in this country to be competitive.

It is keeping you down. It is holding you back. Few things will hinder your professional growth and career advancement more than mediocrity. You do not need new processes. You do not need new equipment. You do not need idealism. To win the battle you merely need to defeat mediocrity.

The workplace is where mediocrity must be defeated. Here is where the battle against apathy, complacency, and indifference must be fought. Here is where you can win the battle against mediocrity. Here is where you must defy mediocrity.

Mediocrity manifests itself in hundreds of ways. Perhaps you might recognize a few. Have you ever heard these words or maybe even spoken them?

"I am not paid to do that. "

"I know nothing about that. "

"It is not my job."

"Someone else will handle that for you."

"That is good enough."

"I can't help you."

"Who cares?"

"Maybe they won't notice the quality problem."

"We can correct that later."

"I'll get to you when I have time."

"Let someone else do that."

"Send it through. The next department will get it."

"That customer was a jerk anyway."

"Who do they think they are, anyway?"

"I am on my break."

"I will sell them the first thing they will buy even if something else might do the job more effectively for them."

"That repair will hold for now. Call us if it breaks again."

"It's not my problem. Someone else caused that problem. Call them."

"I do not like them anyway. The hell with them."

"Who cares what they want?"

"Just throw that box over there, someone else will check it later."

"Someone has a problem. I'm glad it is not me."

"That's not my department."

"I'm out to lunch."

"That is not my responsibility."

I am sure you have dealt with co-workers, clerks, customer service people, and hundreds of others who have spoken these words or very similar ones. Or at least made you feel they were thinking them.

But mediocrity in the work place is not demonstrated with words alone. Mediocrity is both verbal and non-verbal. It is demonstrated by actions, inactions, words, and deeds.

"The only time some people work like a horse is when the boss rides them."
Gabriel Heatter

I have worked with many people who seem to put up invisible shields around them. It is like they are surrounded by a force field whenever you request they take the extra step, cross train, stay late, take on added work, make things easier for others, or do anything outside of what they think they should do. What they think they should do, of course, is the bare minimum needed to keep their job.

You will notice I did not say to do the job right. I said to keep their job. These people are the embodiment of mediocrity. Not embracing these things represents mediocrity. Omission of activity represents mediocrity. Mediocrity manifests itself in a thousand and one ways. Perhaps you recognize a few of these.

The salesclerk who doesn't greet you when you come into the store, or ask if she or he can help you, or thank you for your business?

How about those employees who refuse to pick up a ringing phone, as though they have a broken arm?

Or the salesperson who turns orders in that are missing information and barely legible and assumes someone else will fill in the blanks?

How about the receptionist who greets you rudely and transfers you to the wrong department or disconnects you?

What about the person who promises to do something and then does not do it?

How about the waitress or waiter who brings your meal and never asks if you need anything else and never checks back with you to see if everything was satisfactory?

Or the waiter or waitress who turns you into a waiter by making you sit for 25 minutes waiting for a check?

How about the union worker who hides behind union rules to avoid the pursuit of excellence?

What about those that never return your calls?

How about the production worker who never checks the quality of what they are producing or packing?

How about the cleaning person who vacuums only every other week even though they are being paid to do it every week?

How about the person who accepts no responsibility for anything and seeks to claim credit while assessing blame?

How about people who hide behind voice mail?

What about the employee that stands around the time clock waiting for it to click to the next minute before punching out?

Or the workers who flee the building at 4:30 as though it was on fire no matter how many phones are ringing or how much work is left undone?

How about the employee who pours the last cup of coffee and leaves the empty pot for someone else to clean out and refill?

What about taking care of personal business on company time?

Have you ever waited for help while a clerk was talking on the phone engaged in an obviously personal call on company time?

How about those who assume instead of asking?

How about the salesperson who never follows up on a lead?

How about the person who never pays any attention to details?

What about the employee who is too busy playing politics to do the job?

I could list thousands of examples of mediocrity in action and I would not even be scratching the surface. It surrounds you. You must deal with it every day in hundreds of small and large ways. You must not become part of it. You must not allow it to drag you down. You should never swim in the sea of mediocrity that surrounds you. You must rise above it.

That is the objective of this book. I want to show you how to rise above mediocrity by defying it. We will cover these areas and many others in this brief, **but powerful,** book about defying mediocrity. Along the way I will shatter a few myths that can cause you to embrace an attitude of mediocrity and think it is justified.

Let me assure you mediocrity is a very easy enemy to defeat. In fact, few enemies in your life will be easier to claim victory over then mediocrity. But very few will ever even enter into battle against this truly weak opponent. I hope to change this by showing you how easy it is to defy mediocrity.

Let's get started.

Chapter 2. The company owes me!

"Don't go around saying the world owes you a living; the world owes you nothing; it was here first."

Mark Twain

Ahh, the attitude of entitlement. A lifelong friend of mediocrity. Let's tackle this career killing attitude right now. Let me warn you once again, I will not sugar-coat anything I tell you. I have an obligation to tell you the truth. You deserve nothing less and will get nothing less from me.

With this said, let me confront this often uttered argument head on. **The company owes you nothing but a paycheck for the work you have done.** They have no obligation to take care of you for life. They do not owe you a lifetime job. You owe them an honest day's work and they owe you a paycheck for the wage you agreed to work for. Few formulas are simpler than this.

Also remember that the company pays you when you are out sick. They pay you when you do a mediocre job. They pay you when you are on vacation. They pay you when you make mistakes. They also provide you numerous very costly benefits and a place to grow and advance. They do not owe these latter things. They provide them to you. It is up to you to make the most of them.

Countless times I have heard employees state how they felt the company owed them more. How the company has an obligation to provide for them for life. How the company had a debt to them.

I have spoken with many who have been laid off after years of employment and felt the bitterness and the self-pity of their words. I have interviewed dozens of men and women who found themselves out of a job after a plant or company closed down and listened to the anger and resentment that they harbor toward the company for the predicament they found themselves in.

Think about this. They blamed the company for closing the doors. As though they somehow expected the company to continue losing money solely to provide them a job. They blamed the company for the fact that they had no job as though somehow the company had an obligation to provide the employee a job for as long as the employee wanted one regardless of the employee's value or the company's ability to keep the employee on the payroll. As though these were minor details.

These same employees are the ones who would think nothing of moving to another company for more money in a heartbeat.

They complained about the fact they had spent years working for the company and now feel they have a limited future as they gave so much and so many years to the company as though this meant the company now owed them. Did the company not do its part by paying them every week? Was this not the sole obligation of the company? Did the company agree to provide a job to these employees for life?

If they were laid off or let go because they did not have the skills needed to remain an effective and contributing employee in the current workplace they blamed the company. Did the employee not have a responsibility to obtain the added education and training they needed to keep up with the changes? Why did these people not take the initiative and learn the skills they needed to keep up or, better yet, to make themselves more valuable to the company ?

What happened to the self-responsibility of these people? Are we not all responsible for our own actions and inactions? I know this is not a very popular position to take today. I know that few take responsibility for anything today. I know that all problems are always caused by someone else in today's world. Is it any wonder we are surrounded by mediocrity?

Let me ask you something. If you knew you were going to work for a company for 5, 10, 15, 20, or 25 years or more and then be out of a job would you not use this time to plan for the day you would be out of work? Would you not develop other skills and interests so you would be prepared for the day of unemployment? Would you not plan fiscally as well? Of course you would. If you did not you would have no one to blame but yourself.

Derrick W. Welch

Then why do so many employees think that when they take a job it is forever unless they decide to change positions? Why do they assume the company will take care of them forever unless they decide to leave?

Why do they assume the company will even survive 5, 10, 15, 20, or 25 years? Why do they assume the company will need or be able to afford them in the future? Why do they assume that technology or changing markets or any one of a hundred other changes will not affect their job?

Why do they think the employee / employer relationship is a one-way street with the employee having the options and the employer having some type of obligation that extends infinitely beyond a weekly paycheck? Why do they not realize that changes happen and happen rapidly? Changes that are often forced, unanticipated, and unavoidable. That they, not the company, are responsible for their own future.

Think of someone being employed by the same company for 30 years and then one day being faced with unemployment. If the employee assumed that he would have a job with this company for life, if he assumed the company would need him until he chose to leave, if he assumed the company would be able to afford to keep him until he chose to leave, if he assumed he would never need to improve his skills and capabilities, he would be shocked and unprepared.

But if the employee understood that the future was his responsibility, that the only true obligation the company had was to pay him each week for his efforts, that change could occur anytime and was not always positive, that the company could downsize or even close down one day, that his skills may know longer be needed or affordable, then he could have taken the steps to be prepared.

If he realized his skills might not have kept up with the changes of the business he could have spent his time acquiring new skills. Skills that would make him more valuable to the company instead of expendable. He could have put all his efforts toward making the company as good as he could so it would survive. He could have fiscally prepared for the day that was coming. **Don't let this happen to you. Take responsibility for your future. It is your responsibility, not the company's.**

16

Chapter 3. If you want me to do more, just pay me more.

"The only place where success comes before work is in the dictionary."

Vidal Sassoon

"Pay me more and I will do more. Pay me more and I will do a better job." **The battle cry of mediocrity.**

I know that in many ways this chapter hits on a number of things I have addressed in other chapters. However, it is an area of such importance, and an attitude so often seen, I feel compelled to give this subject a chapter all its own.

A common problem today is that employees want to be paid more to perform better. The problem is that they have this backwards. What they are saying is that if they are paid more they will do a better job. This, of course, means that they are not doing the job as well as they could or should be doing it now. Mediocrity will be defeated only when this attitude changes.

Take a few minutes and think about this. **If you have this attitude what you are saying is that you can do a much better job but only if you are paid more. Perhaps this is why you are not paid more.** Unless you are a professional athlete you are paid based on what you do and what you contribute, not on what you could do or might do.

If you want to earn more then you must increase your value to the company. You must help the company earn more. Look out for the company's interests if you want them to look out for yours.

To earn more you must first prove you are worth more.

You don't get paid what you need. You don't get paid what you want. You shouldn't. You get paid based on your value to your employer. The way it should be. Start giving more and you will start getting more.

Derrick W. Welch

"You must pay the price if you wish to secure the blessings."

Andrew Jackson

You cannot expect to get what you want by first demanding and then performing. Perform first and then expect. Prove you are worth more and you will earn more.

Let me also point out that if you want to earn more many times you must learn more. Many jobs have a preset value to the company. Many jobs, no matter how well done, can only command a specific level of pay. Yes, there will be a range within the pay scale of most jobs and yes, you can earn more by doing a better job. But to earn above the top of the scale you will need to increase your knowledge and capabilities.

To advance to a higher level of earnings you must often move up to a higher level of responsibility. This will often mean learning more. It is up to you to undertake the needed training and education to qualify yourself. It is up to you to gain the qualifications you need to move to a higher level of responsibility and earnings.

But never forget that the ability and capability must come before the opportunity and earnings. The individual in pursuit of excellence understands this. The mind-set of mediocrity does not and by not understanding this they hold themselves back while blaming others for their lack of progress or advancement.

Chapter 4. Your obligation.

"Only by helping others get what they want can you get what you want."

Derrick W. Welch

What is the employee / employer relationship? Lets look at this relationship at its most basic level, remembering we live in a free market, capitalistic society.

Too many employees, and I consider everyone other than the owners an employee including management, have developed the mind-set that the company owes them something.

They are right of course. As I have indicated earlier, the company does owe you something. The company owes you a paycheck for the agreed upon wage. This is the wage that you have agreed to work for. Yes, of course, the company also has an obligation to provide a safe workplace and to provide you with the resources you need to do your job in a manner that allows you to meet or exceed their expectations.

But you also have an obligation. An obligation to your employer to do the very best job you possibly can. Day in and day out this obligation exists. Is this not what you promised to do when you accepted the job? Was this not your intention when you accepted the job? Is the company not paying you for your best effort? I can assure you they expect nothing less. They deserve nothing less.

Every week that you cash a paycheck from your employer you have this obligation.

Is this not a form of a contract? In exchange for your best effort every day the company is agreeing to pay you a preset wage. Few things in life could be simpler than this. You expect to be paid and they expect you to be at the job and to do it in a manner that meets or exceeds their needs and expectations.

Derrick W. Welch

You will notice I said your best effort. They do not decrease or increase your wage each week based on how well you do the job each week. They pay you for your best effort each week.

If you feel you are paid too little for your efforts and accomplishments you can seek more money from your current employer and, if they agree, you will get it. If they disagree with you over what you should be compensated or if they are unable to pay you more, you have the right to see if another firm is willing to pay you what you think your efforts are worth.

What could possibly be simpler than this?

But never forget that as long as you accept a paycheck from your employer you have an obligation to them. An obligation to do the best job you can. An obligation to look out for the company's interests.

You also have an obligation to yourself. An obligation to do the very best job you can. To do otherwise would undermine your self-esteem and professional growth.

You know what? It will also be the best thing you can do for your career.

Chapter 5. There is more than one type of customer service you know.

"I'm not perfect, but I strive for excellence."

Marva Collins

What does the often used, but rarely understood, term "customer service" mean to you? Most people think of customer service as the service given to external customers, customers who buy the products and services of the company.

To many people it refers to the quality of service they give to the customer or they receive from the companies and people they conduct business with. Most people talk about customer service and make wonderful promises and claims about how good the customer service they offer is. But the reality of it is that excellence in the area of customer service is about as rare as free trade in China.

Excellence in customer service means much more than just selling a product or delivering a service with a smile. Excellence in customer service means consistently, day in and day out, customer after customer, delivering a quality product or service in a manner that, at least, meets, and hopefully exceeds, your customer's expectations each and every time.

This is really not a very complex process. However, it is one that is rarely seen in any business today. An attitude of apathy, inconsistency, and complacency are more the norm.

To most of you the term "customer service" means little as you think it only refers to those in the customer service department or those who deal directly with the external customer. Simply put, you think it is not your responsibility. You are wrong. Very wrong!

Yes, excellence in external customer service is important, vitally important. But there is another form of customer service that you must work at improving. I am speaking of internal customer service.

Each of your co-workers and employees is an internal customer. Each department is an internal customer to the other.

Unless you are able to provide top flight internal customer service your company will never be able to provide the best external customer service possible. They will never be able to maximize productivity, improve quality, and increase profitability. Excellence in both areas must be the goal. Any other goal will be very costly. Very costly indeed.

Internal customer service deals with an attitude of assistance among all employees. It deals with each employee, no matter how high up or how low down the corporate ladder, making sure they have not made an error or assumption that is being passed on to the next person or department. It deals with asking and not assuming. It deals with you and each of your co-workers doing all that you can to facilitate the overall objectives of the company and not just your individual objectives.

Internal customer service deals with reducing errors in all departments. It deals with clear and effective communication. It means thinking about how you can make the job of others easier, not how to make your own job easier. It means going the extra step and striving for excellence in everything you do.

It means functioning as a team and not just talking about it. It means treating others as you would like to be treated. It means always striving to exceed the expectations of your co-workers and of other departments.

Internal customer service deals with a commitment, a commitment to doing the best job that can be done the first time. It deals with being careful and not careless. It must start with the initial customer contact and continues through to the delivery of your product or service.

The attitude of "it is not my job" or "let someone else worry about that" has no place in a company driven to provide outstanding customer service. **It should have no place in your company.**

Defy Mediocrity: The Employee's 90 Minute Guide To Excellence

To achieve excellence in the area of internal customer service your mind-set has got to be "How can I help you?" "How can I make your job easier?" "How can I make the job of the next person in the process easier?" If everyone thinks like this each of you will be looking out for each other.

Notice I said your mind-set and you. Not someone else but you. You must think this way. You can't wait for someone else to think this way and act this way towards you. You must start thinking and acting this way.

"To be the best you can you must always give the best you have. Nothing else should ever be acceptable to you."

Derrick W. Welch

You must think "How can I do my job so well and so far above what is expected that I can make your job easier?" If you are thinking this while the other employees are thinking the same thing how much better do you think your company will be? How much more effective do you think you will be? How much do you think your product, process, performance, and service will improve? How much more enjoyable do you think your job would be? How much better do you think your company will be?

Think of the cycle of goodwill you will be creating. The cycle of helpfulness. The cycle of looking out for each other, of correcting each other's mistakes and oversights. The atmosphere of teamwork. The sense of comradery.

You will be amazed at the positive feelings you will generate and receive working in this manner, with this mind-set. Your sense of job satisfaction will increase dramatically, as will the sense of job satisfaction of those around you.

Think of how much better your external service would be. Think of how much wasted time would be recovered and reallocated to more productive and profitable efforts.

Poor internal customer service costs the company money in hundreds of different ways. From quality problems to operational delays and redundancies, poor internal customer service costs money. It will also cause serious morale problems and severely hinders the company's ability to provide exceptional external customer service.

It limits the company's ability to be competitive. We will talk about this more later, but let me also point out that <u>if it is bad for the company it is bad for the employees.</u> If it costs the company money it hinders the company's ability to pay you more, to provide better working conditions, to upgrade equipment, and to provide better benefits.

Think of excellence in internal service as a critical piece of the puzzle. The puzzle that makes a mediocre employee great and turns a bad company into a good company and a good company into a great company. It cannot be accomplished without you!

Chapter 6. If you want to work for a great company, start by becoming a great employee.

"It is not enough to see the possibility, you must become the possibility."

Dr. Robert Anthony

People create the perception of a company. Your customers view your company a certain way as a result of their contact with you. Your co-workers perceive the company a certain way because of their contact with you. The corporation is a cold intangible organization. People create positive morale. Good people improve morale because others enjoy working with them and for them. Bad people destroy morale because co-workers dislike working with them or for them.

How would you like it if your co-workers took bogus sick days, made inexcusable mistakes, passed half assed jobs onto you, and undertook any one of a hundred other unacceptable activities? Your negative feelings toward these people affect your feelings to the company.

You wonder why they are allowed to do this. You question management behind their backs. You become dissatisfied with your job because you are doing things you should not need to do.

In a case like this you can work for the greatest company in the world and you will hate your job and hate the company.

People enjoy their jobs because of the people they work with. If you did not enjoy working with the people at your company, you would not enjoy your job no matter how much you might enjoy the work. If you do not enjoy your job, what do you think your feelings about the company will be?

Do you think you would feel that the company was a great company if you did not enjoy your job? How could you?

Derrick W. Welch

"The best way to work with outstanding people is to become one."

Derrick W. Welch

But the problem is not the company, it is people. Don't be one of them. People are what make the difference in a company. Great employees are what create a great company.

Treat others with the respect and professionalism you want from them. Set the example. Set the standard. It starts with you, not them. Perform the way you want others to. Do not take the attitude that you will when they do. They will have the same "the heck with them" attitude. This turns into a self-perpetuating, self-defeating cycle of mediocrity.

It must start with you. Lead the way. Don't wait for others so you can follow.

Chapter 7. Your actions speak so loud I do not need to hear your words.

"We are what we repeatedly do. Excellence, then, is not an act, but a habit."

Aristotle

You can't buy a reputation, you must build one. You can't command loyalty, you must earn it. You can't be given respect, you must earn it. Respect from your customers. Respect from your co-workers, respect from your employees, respect from your boss.

"The quality of an individual is reflected in the standards they set for themselves."

Ray Kroc

You must set the standard. People will follow your actions not your words. If you demand they do one thing while you do another, which do you think others will mirror? If you preach cost control, increased productivity, honesty, and integrity and then take time off from work on false pretenses, use company labor and materials for personal projects, what do you think others will do?

You will be laying a foundation of abuse, dishonesty, lack of integrity, and poor morale. If you do not care or do not live by the rules you expect them to, neither will they. Your actions cause a reaction.

You must lead by example. How can you expect others to adhere to the policies if you do not? How can you ask for honesty if you do not demonstrate it? How can you arrive late every day while demanding others come in on time? How can you expect others to act ethically when you do not?

How can you expect others to go out of their way to help you when you do nothing to help them? How can you ask others to improve quality when you do nothing to improve your own? How can you expect the best effort every day from others when you do not give your best effort every day?

Treat your co-workers the way you would like to be treated even if they do not treat you that way.

Never expect someone else to live up to standards that you are unwilling or unable to live up to. You must set the example. **The attitude of "I will when they do" is unacceptable. This lowers yourself to a level below your capabilities. This is the attitude of mediocrity.**

You set the expectations by your deeds and words. This goes both for managers and their employees as well as for employees and their co-workers.

> *"Example is not the main thing in influencing others. It is the only thing."*
>
> *Albert Schweitzer*

You must walk the talk. You cannot say one thing and do another. Doing so will be the end of any efforts by anyone else. Showing me means something. Telling me means little.

If you do not demonstrate the commitment, your co-workers never will. **It must start with you**. Not someone else, but you. Think about how destructive and ineffective it is to others who dedicate themselves to a program of internal customer service or any other job improvement performance efforts while you embrace your own program of mediocrity.

It will not work. It will create resentment. I have seen it happen first hand. **All efforts to improve will be doomed if you are not committed.**

Others will follow your lead. The defeat of mediocrity can become infectious. It starts with you. Others will mirror your example. Good or bad.

> *"As I grow older I pay less attention to what they say. I just watch what they do."*
>
> *Andrew Carnegie*

You can't expect others to consider your needs if you do not consider theirs. You can't expect your co-workers to give 100% to all they do while you put forth no more than the minimum effort. You can't expect your boss to consider you for a promotion or increased responsibility if you are not a team player who does all he or she can do to help others and to help the department and company accomplish its goals.

You can't complain about others coming in late when you leave early. You can't demand others work extra hours when you don't. You can't expect co-workers to do all they can to make your job easier when you do nothing or very little to make their's easier.

You can't take company supplies and question the honesty of others. You can't take long lunches and then wonder why others won't skip a break to help you out.

You can't put personal agendas and activities ahead of corporate objectives and then complain that you are not getting further up the corporate ladder. You might think you can, but you are wrong! **We are talking about show and tell**. You cannot talk about and expect one thing and show them something else. You might like to think you can, but you are wrong. Do not be naive. People will do as you do, not as you say.

> *"It is commitment, not authority that produces results."*
>
> *William L. Gore*

Your co-workers or employees will not bust their butts to do a better job while you do not. Instead of developing a common goal and improving morale, you will have poor morale, resentment, and an attitude of "the hell with them". You will create dissension and foster an "us against them" mentality. How can you expect commitment from anyone else if you do not demonstrate it? How long would you shovel sand in the ocean?

"You must demonstrate commitment before you can demand it. "

Derrick W. Welch

Excellence has a price. The price is commitment. Without commitment you will never achieve excellence. Make no mistake about it. You can't state what you want and do nothing about it. You can't claim to be committed to your company, to self-improvement, and to excellence in the area of internal customer service while you look out for your own interests only.

You cannot have it both ways. **You are either committed to excellence or you are not.**

Chapter 8. Excuses. We all have them.

"We don't need more strength or more ability or greater opportunity. What we need is to use what we have."

Basil S. Walsh

Excuses are often the bane of the weak. They give us reasons for failing or not even trying. They are the food that feeds our fragile egos. They allow us to justify what we do or do not do. Excuses. We all have them.

Too big. Too small. Black. White. Man. Woman. Short. Tall. Fat. Thin. Attractive. Unattractive. Well educated. High School drop out. Well connected. Not connected. High I.Q. . Low I.Q. .

<u>Excuses are very easy to come by. But make no mistake about it, most are nothing more than self-justification for failure or unaccomplished objectives.</u> In short, most are just bull! Excuses. That is all they are. Excuses. They will never represent an acceptable reason for not doing the best job you can day in and day out.

"Always bear in mind that your own resolution to succeed is more important than any other thing."

Abraham Lincoln

Men and women with far less going for them than you and I, have accomplished far more than we might even dare to dream about. Think about this. The average person's I.Q. is around 100. An I.Q. of over 160 qualifies you as a genius.

Imagine that. A genius is only 60% smarter, according to the experts, than the average person. In other words, if you can read this book, a genius could not possibly be even twice as smart as you are. So how can so many accomplish so much more than others?

How can some men make millions of dollars a year while others make a few thousand? How, then, can one person be so much more successful than another? Clearly it is not due to the difference in intelligence between them. How can this be?

Let me give you the answer. Your commitment and effort will always be more important than your I.Q..

"Nothing in the world can take the place of persistence. Talent will not; nothing is more common than unsuccessful men with talent. Genius will not; unrewarded genius is almost a proverb. Education will not; the world is full of educated derelicts. Persistence and determination alone are omnipotent."

Calvin Coolidge

Stop looking for excuses and start figuring out how to improve your results. Stop thinking why you can't or won't and start justifying why you can and how you will. Start putting your best effort forth each day.

"If we did all the things we are capable of doing we would literally astound ourselves."

Thomas Edison

These words from a man with less than three months of "formal schooling". An exception? Hardly. Henry Ford had less than 6 years of "formal education". William Gates dropped out of Harvard. These men and countless others like them knew results are what count in life, not excuses. Education and academic credentials will never be a substitute for common sense and an unwavering commitment to your job.

How about Jim Abbott the outstanding pitcher for the Chicago White Sox? What is so special about Jim Abbott? He was born with only one hand! **He has defied all the odds in his pursuit of individual excellence.**

"The difference between a successful person and others is not a lack of strength, not a lack of knowledge, but rather a lack of will."

Vince Lombardi

Settling is always easy to do and simple to justify. Doing less than you could or should will always be an easy path to justify. Excuses come to mind far quicker than reasons why you should do a better job with the project at hand. <u>Excuses pave the path to mediocrity.</u>

But the easy way out is often copping out. You are sending a message to yourself and those around you. A message of mediocrity. Just resign yourself to failure. Don't try. Why bother? You will only fail. What other choice do you have?

Well, the only other choice would seem to be to succeed. To improve. To perform your best day in and day out.

"If you argue for your limitations you get to keep them."

Dr. Robert Anthony

The choice is yours to make.

Chapter 9. Questions are the key to the door of improvement.

"Why and how are words so important that they cannot be too often used."

Napoleon

It was Kipling who gave us what was perhaps the greatest advice for business success and, in fact, success in life, that has ever been given. He told us the key to success in all areas when he said **"I had six honest serving men. They taught me all I knew. Their names were: where and what and when and why and how and who.".**

The late great Earl Nightingale suggested we add two more friends to this group. They are, which and if. I suggest you add as many more as you can to this group.

Whatever type of improvement you are seeking, questions will provide the answers. Whether you are seeking to find ways to increase sales or control and reduce costs, questions are the key. Whether you are striving to improve your customer service or the quality of your product, questions are the key.

Whether you are seeking to find ways to improve yourself or your job-related performance, questions will show you the way.

Asking the questions and developing the answers are the keys to any and all success you will have in business and, in fact, in life.

Questions like:

Which is better?
If we make that purchase what is the payback period?
If we do this what happens?
Why do we do it that way?
Why do we not do it that way?
What if we tried this?
Why do we need this?

Why do we buy that many?
Why do we buy that few?
Why do we need it?
Why can't we do without it?
Why do we not buy more to save on the unit cost?
What are we planning to do with them?
Why do we only get one bid?
Why are we paying that much?
Why do we not deal with another company?
Why do we do this at all?
What does this add?
Is this effort cost justified?
What can we do to reduce costs?
What can I do to improve productivity?
What can I do to improve quality?
What can I do to improve our service?
What can I do to improve myself?
What steps can we take to streamline?
When do we do that? Why?
How else can we do this function?
How else can that be done?
How can we do it better, faster, cheaper?
How can I do my job better?
How can we improve quality, service, profits?
How can we reduce waste?
How can we sell more to that customer?
How can we cut costs?
How can I make things easier for the next department?
Is there a better way? There always is!
If we do not do that what happens?
If we do this will we improve quality?
If we do this will it improve service?
If we do this will it increase profits?
If we do this will it save time?
Which is better? Why?
Which provides us with better quality?
Which is best for our customer?
Will this process or step add value to our product or service or does it produce added profit?

You see my point, I am sure. You must ask questions and seek out the answers. You must also justify the answers. **You must never stop asking. If you are not continuously asking the questions and reacting to the answers you are either assuming or stagnating. Either one can be deadly to your career and your company.**

"I do not believe you can do today's job with yesterday's methods and still be in business tomorrow."

Nelson Jackson

Questions are also the key to improvements in every area of your job performance and your company. Do you know how your products are produced and distributed? Do you know what goes into your product or service? I don't mean a general idea, I mean specifics.

Is your product flow or order processing set up to maximize time, quality, and productivity and reduce costs? If you don't know, how can you expect to control costs, improve or control quality, and improve productivity? How can you expect to find a better way to do your job if you don't know how things are done now and how your efforts impact them? Why do you do these things this way? How can you find a better way if you don't know how it is being done now and why?

"The one real objective of education is to have a man in the condition of continually asking questions."

Bishop Mandell Creighton

Examine every single area that you are involved in Every single area. There are very few areas in which you cannot improve. You must find ways to eliminate needless steps, improve productivity, reduce errors, increase sales, reduce expenses, improve service, and improve quality.

"There is a better way for everything. Find it."

Thomas Edison

Always strive for improvement in everything you do. Tom Peters once said "Do 1,000 things just 1% better and soon you'll be 1,000 % better.". He is right. Numerous small improvements will equate to major improvements. The Japanese call this type of management thinking "Kaizen". A more radical version of this type of thinking is popularly known in this country as "reengineering". Call it what you will, it does not matter, just adopt this type of thinking.

You must always be asking yourself if this is the best you can do. **The quest for improvement must be never-ending. But you will never be able to do this unless you ask the questions.** Why do you do what you do the way you do it? Why do you not do it another way? **Ask the questions. They are the key to the door of improvement.**

"If you are satisfied with the best you have done you will never do the best you can."

Martin VanBee

Never assume you can't do better. Always assume you can do better. From the way you do things to the way you work with others, it is up to you to improve things. Improvement is always possible in everything we do.

It is not up to someone else. It is up to you.

Forget the way it has always been done. Forget the fancy names like "reengineering" and "Kaizen". Use your God given common sense. You possess the greatest thinking machine ever created and it sits right between your two ears. You own it, free and clear. All you need to do is put it to work.

Chapter 10. Appearance does count.

"Don't complain about the snow on your neighbor's roof when your own doorstep is unclean."

Confucius

Appearance is important. Very important. Whether it be your personal appearance or the appearance of the area you work in for so many hours each day. It is a link in the overall chain. The chain of change that you will use to defy mediocrity.

Make sure that all areas you work in are kept clean and professional. I am not just speaking to those of you who work in the showroom or lobby. Whether you work in the warehouse, loading dock, front office, or boardroom, I am speaking to you.

It doesn't matter if you do not have a single customer or outsider ever visit your facility or work area. The condition of the area you occupy in your company speaks volumes about you and the pride or lack of pride you take in your work.

A clean and polished work area makes a statement about your work habits, personal pride, and the quality of your product or service. It is a marketing tool. It provides for a safer workplace. It forces you and your co-workers to take pride in what you do and where you do it. It will help you to keep your equipment well maintained and presentable and it sets a standard that will be carried over to all areas of the company .

You will feel better about coming to work each day. You will take pride when others see your work area. You will work safer, you will produce better quality, and you will be more productive.

The details do make a difference. They always do!

Chapter 11. Real improvement must start with the person in the mirror.

"Don't measure yourself by what you have accomplished, but by what you should have accomplished with your ability."

John Wooden

Self-improvement and self-assessment are critical to your quest to defy mediocrity. You must constantly be asking yourself the questions. How can you become better at what you do? What do you need to do or learn to become better? Where can you find the knowledge, information, and education you need to improve?

In what areas are you strong and in what areas are you weak? You must be honest with yourself. No one is ever as good at their job as they can be and should be. We can all become better at what we do and how we do it.

To think otherwise results in complacency and stagnation. Two good friends of mediocrity. We can all learn more. Education must be a never-ending process. If you are still getting by on what you learned in school, you are probably doing just that. Just getting by.

A high school or college degree from years ago may be of limited value to you today. Everything changes. You must constantly increase your knowledge if you are to not just keep up, but to excel.

What you learned from a textbook may have very little value to you on the job. What you learned years ago may be of limited use to you today. Twenty years ago, heck even five years ago, they could not have possibly taught you what you need to know today.

How could they have? They could never have known about the advances that have been made or the changes in the workplace.

They could never have known about what you are doing now and want to be doing tomorrow. They could never have known about your employer's expectations. Knowledge must be evolutionary. Today's knowledge and techniques may be outdated tomorrow.

"Knowledge is the pavement on the path to excellence."

Derrick W. Welch

The defeat of mediocrity is the pursuit of excellence. Learning and education should be a lifelong process. It should never end. **All too many think that graduation is the end of learning. They could not be more wrong. They think that the commencement ceremony marks the end of learning. Look up this word sometime and you will see that commencement means the beginning not the end.**

Understand, I am not talking just about the continuation of your education on a formal basis. Your continuing education can be in a formal setting or an informal one.

It doesn't matter as long as you continue the learning process. When we stop learning we stop growing. We stop stretching ourselves. We stop asking questions. If our quest for knowledge was not insatiable we might still be living in caves.

Stop learning and you embrace mediocrity. Stop seeking to increase your knowledge and you stop thinking and become a robot. You simply go through the motions each day. Stop learning, asking, and questioning and you might as well stop living.

"I don't think much of a man who is not wiser today than he was yesterday."

Abraham Lincoln

How much better do you think you will be at your job if you are using the same techniques as you used last year, or 5 years ago? Not much better I assure you.

Learn from others. Learn from books. Learn from seminars. Learn from tapes. Learn from trying. Learn from your mistakes. Learn from trade magazines. Learn from trade shows.

When a company sells a product or service, they sell it in the marketplace against competition. To get customers to purchase from them they try to differentiate themselves and position their product or service as not just different, but better. Better priced, better quality, better service or any one of dozens of ways to demonstrate that somehow their product is superior to that of the competition and will do a better job of meeting the needs of the prospect.

It is no different with you. You are your own product. You must constantly be improving your product.

What is that you say? You don't have time? <u>Nonsense</u>. This is a classic excuse. And, like most excuses, it is baloney.

Think about this. If you dedicate even one hour a day to learning more about your industry, improving your skills, thinking of ways to do your job better, to help others do their job better, of how to improve the company, the products and services your company puts out, to improve customer service, or to developing new products, you will be dedicating 365 hours per year solely to improvement.

This is equal to over 9 full time weeks of work. Over two full months a year that can easily be dedicated to improving your knowledge and capability. <u>Think of how much better you can become and how much you can advance your career and help your company with this amount of time dedicated solely to your goal of improvement.</u> All this from only one hour per day.

If you tell me you can't spare even one hour a day to improve yourself and increase your knowledge and value, you are simply wrapping yourself in a cloak of mediocrity made of excuses.

Think of how much time you spend sitting in front of the television set each night. I can assure you for most people it is far more than one hour per night.

"Acquire new knowledge whilst thinking over the old, and you may become a teacher of others."

Confucius

Everything changes. Change brings with it opportunity. You must change to realize the opportunities change creates and provides. One hour per day dedicated to self-assessment and self-improvement will produce astounding results. You will be engaging in a process that few others ever will.

Now think about spending 2 hours per day or over 4 months per year to this process. How long do you thing it would take you to reach the level of capability you are seeking?

You will be amazed at how much better you can become at what you do simply by spending a little time each day asking yourself the questions and acting on the answers.

Stop looking for excuses and start finding solutions.

Chapter 12. The good of the company must always take precedence over the good of the individual.

"Things that are bad for business are bad for the people who work for business."

Thomas Dewey

Now, I know you might not like hearing this but it is true. As I have told you before, you will hear no idealistic, socialistic, academic nonsense from me in anything I write. The plain simple truth is that the company must come before the individual. If the company cannot survive and prosper they have no need of you or I.

"The basic need of every company is to make a profit. Only then can it provide jobs and earnings for employees."

I.W. Abel
Former President - United Steelworkers of America

If the company can't make a profit, how are they going to pay you? Clearly there is a direct link in your ability to accomplish your career goals and the company's ability to reach theirs.

Decisions often must be made to protect the interest of the company. Decisions you may not always like. If the company does not produce adequate profits what is the point of staying in business? Things must often be done to protect the long and short term interest of the company. Things you may or may not see, understand, or agree with.

We do not live in a socialistic society although at times it may seem that way and it has been suggested that many government leaders of this country might like that. But the fact is we live in a free market economy. We function under a form of limited capitalism.

Derrick W. Welch

For a business to function in our society it must make an acceptable level of profit. What is acceptable? That is up to the owners, including stockholders, of that business. They are the ones taking the risk. They are the ones that stand to lose should the business venture fail. They face the losses. They face the lawsuits. They pay the bills. They stay up sleepless at night. They have the liability.

They have the right to decide what is an acceptable level of profit and what is not. They have the right to decide at what point the profit is so low that they should liquidate the company and invest their money in some other investment. Some other investment without the incredible risk and headaches that go along with running a business today.

You can't decide this. I can't decide this. If we feel our pay is too low and profits are too high we have the option of finding another job more suitable to our perception of what is fair.

It is not the company's obligation to pay me what I think I deserve or what I may need. This is the attitude of entitlement. The attitude of mediocrity.

They will, and should, only compensate me at a level they feel is required to keep me at that job. If I want to earn more I must increase my value to the company.

We have no right to determine that we should be paid more because profits are "too high". Some academics and some in the government may feel they or other non risk taking owners can determine what is right and wrong or how much is too much, but they are wrong.

They have no right to decide this. They are not taking the risk and responsibility of running the business.

Chapter 13. Change. It is inescapable.

"Those who say the only certain things in life are death and taxes are wrong. They have forgotten about change."

Derrick W. Welch

Let's talk about change. Don't like the newest change at the company? Think the strategy is the wrong one? Don't like the new product line? Don't agree with the latest promotion or consolidation?

Well let me give you a hard hitting news flash. It is your job to support it. To support the new change, the new direction, the new boss. It is your job to sell the new product line, meet the new quota, help implement the new strategy.

"The most effective way to cope with change is to help create it."

L.W. Lynett

Yes, of course, you should provide input whenever you can to improve things, to make the new change even better. Yes, of course, you should speak out if you think management has overlooked something. If possible, try to have input into the process that determines the change. Your thoughts, ideas, input, and even objections can prove very valuable. But at some point the decision is made. The time to object and provide input is past.

Once the change has been made and any and all modifications to it have been made, it is your job to support it, to help make it successful.

You may not always be able to see the overall or big picture. You only have to consider a small piece of the overall puzzle. You may not need to consider today and tomorrow. The owners and management of the company must think short and long term.

They must look at the big picture. You may just be a small, albeit very important, piece of the overall puzzle.

You may not be able to see how all the pieces fit together. Those in charge must tend to the health and prosperity of the whole and this may not always be pleasant to you and the reason for many of the strategies employed may not be sensible or logical to you or even apparent to you.

What is that you say? You don't agree? Well let me ask you "are you still coming to work everyday and collecting a paycheck?" You are? Well, then it is your job to support the plan, program, or boss. This is what your company is asking you do to and paying you to do.

They are not paying you to disagree or to bad mouth the company or the company's plans. They are paying you to help them succeed. If you can't or won't, they do not need you.

Think of this as a sports team. Someone calls the play. You might not like the play. You might think it is the wrong call. You might be completely convinced it is a bad call. But guess what? You have a responsibility to do all you can to make that play work. It is your job. It is what you are being paid for.

If you are not helping the team succeed, you are helping ensure they won't. No company will ever pay you to help them fail.

While you are with your employer it is your responsibility, and indeed your obligation (you are still cashing those paychecks aren't you?), to support, or at least not fight, the direction of the company.

It can't succeed without your efforts and support.

Chapter 14. Deal with things the way they are, not the way you would like them to be or think they should be.

"Faced with the choice between changing one's mind and proving that there is no need to do so, almost everybody gets busy on the proof."

John Kenneth Galbraith

Swimming against the tide will never get you to your destination. At the very least it will take far longer to get there. You must deal with the way things are, not the way you would like them to be.

You must strive to become the best you can within the framework of the organization you work for. If you can't or won't, you have a right, and indeed an obligation, to yourself and your employer, to find an organization offering you the framework you are seeking.

Never forget that you must deal with things the way they are. Not the way you want them to be. Not the way you think they should be. The way they are.

"People are always blaming their circumstances for what they are. I don't believe in circumstances. The people who get on in this world are the people who get up and look for the circumstances they want, and, if they can't find them, make them."

George Bernard Shaw

Spending time moaning and complaining about things because you think they should be different will get you nowhere and could severely hinder every area of your career. It can destroy your enthusiasm and morale. It could give you a bad reputation. It could brand you as a troublemaker and a problem employee.

It will cloud your judgment and make others not want to work with you, never mind help you.

You can't always control your circumstances or the situations that arise. But you can always control your reaction to them.

You control your emotions and your reactions. Who else could? You can control your anger, frustration, acceptance. **What happens to you and around you is sometimes beyond your control, but never forget that how you react to the situation is always under you control.**

Chapter 15. Responsibility. It seems to be a forgotten word today, unless, of course, it is someone else's.

"99% responsibility doesn't work."

Dr. Robert Anthony

What do you do when you make a mistake? Do you try to cover it up or correct it before anyone finds out? Do you try to shift the blame to someone else? Do you defend your actions instead of admitting your error?

"A man who commits a mistake and doesn't correct it is committing another mistake."

Confucius

When you make a mistake and do anything but admit it, correct it if possible, and learn from it, you are making another mistake. If you have not done something you should have, admit it and do the thing you should have done.

People will respect you for admitting you are not perfect. Your co-workers and superiors will respect you for your willingness to step forward and admit you have made a mistake.

If you defend your actions, deny your mistake, or try to shift responsibility for something that was clearly your mistake, you will earn nothing but distrust and disdain.

No one is perfect. There is no one who has never made a mistake. If anyone tells me this they are either lying or not doing much of anything. I would not want to work with either.

You have many responsibilities in your job. Sometimes you will succeed at each and sometime you will screw up. That is life.

The goal is to correct your mistake if possible, learn from it, and move on without repeating it again.

When you start accepting responsibility for your actions and inactions that is when you are defying mediocrity. If you do anything else you are embracing mediocrity.

One of the most important tools you can have is a mirror. When you want to find out why you have not improved to the level you want to, this is when you will want to look in the mirror. Stop blaming circumstances or others. Start taking responsibility.

"The price of greatness is responsibility."

Winston Churchill

What do you do when you see something that needs to be done but you don't want to do it? Do you pretend not to know about it? Do you pretend you do not hear the phone ringing? Do you pretend not to notice the deed that needs to be done?

If so, let me ask you who you think you are kidding? Most often others know you had the opportunity to do what needed to be done and you did not do it. They know you pretended not to see or know about what needed to be done. They know you defied not mediocrity, but excellence. They know you left the task for someone else to do. They know you pretended.

What do you think they will think about you? How much do you think they will want to help you? Even if no one else knows, you know. You know what you did was wrong. You know you embraced mediocrity.

If it is not my responsibility and it is not your responsibility, whose responsibility is it? Don't run from responsibility. This is one battle against mediocrity that you can win very easily.

Chapter 16. Who is watching anyway?

"Whenever you are to do a thing, though it can never be known but to yourself, ask yourself how you would act were all the world looking at you, and act accordingly."

Thomas Jefferson

Do you ever wonder if your efforts are appreciated or even noticed? One of the greatest failings of today's managers is that they do not provide adequate feedback, positive or negative, to the people that work for them. This is a very unfortunate and foolish situation and will be a subject of a future book. But, for now, I want to focus on you and how you can pursue excellence and not the shortcomings of others.

Because you may not receive consistent feedback regarding your efforts you may often wonder whether management or even co-workers even notice what you do. You may wonder how important your efforts are and you might think that little impact will be made even if you dramatically improve your performance.

"You have to perform at a consistently higher level than others. That's the mark of a true professional."

Joe Paterno

Ask yourself this. Could you do a better job and are not simply because you think your efforts are not being noticed?

If so, perhaps this is the reason you are not getting ahead faster. Perhaps your efforts are being noticed and you may be in position for a promotion or raise and you do not even know it.

Can you afford to take a chance? You never know who is watching.

Derrick W. Welch

For those of you who work harder when you think someone is watching or paying attention and shift back into lower gear when you think no one is watching let me give you a tip.

You are kidding yourself. It is foolish to think you can know when you are being observed or that others do not know what you are or are not doing. You never know. You may think they do not notice subpar efforts but you are wrong.

Someone will always notice your efforts, excellent or poor. Never forget that many others will see the results of your efforts or the lack of results you produce. From the people in the next department to the customer who uses your products.

Furthermore, think about this. **Is your goal not to be noticed? If so, you are the embodiment of mediocrity. This book was written for you. Not someone else, you.**

You should always be doing the best you can. To do otherwise is inexcusable and should always be unacceptable. Take some pride in what you do.

Live up to your contract with your employer. What contract? The contract that you enter into every time you cash that paycheck they are paying you for your best effort.

Not just when you think they are watching. How would you like to get paid only when you think someone notices your efforts? You want to get a days pay and your employer deserves nothing less than a days work.

Let me also remind you there is one person who is always watching. One who always sees what you do and do not do and how well you do it. One person who uses the standard you set on the job as an example for all other areas of their life.

Who is this all-seeing person? The person in the mirror. You can never hide from yourself.

You know that you are engaging in a behavior that is self-defeating and will doom you to an existence of mediocrity. You are forming habits that will guarantee that you always perform at a level of mediocrity or lower.

Chapter 17. If you want to be recognized and appreciated, make sure you are recognizing others and showing your appreciation.

"The deepest desire in human nature is the desire to feel important."

Doctor John Dewey

One way to foster positive feelings from others is to do what you can to help them and to thank them. Just as it is critical to thank your customers, it is equally important to thank your co-workers. They are your internal customers.

Let them know how much you appreciate their efforts. They will want to work hard to gain this type of honest sincere appreciation. Wouldn't you?

If they think you don't care, how much do you think they will care? How hard do you think they will work to help you? They will work much harder for someone that they like and who appreciates what they do than they will for someone who threatens, complains, ignores, or shows no appreciation. Wouldn't you?

This goes for both management and employees to other employees. Build relationships. Make the jobs of others easier so they will help make your job easier.

Build support among your people and co-workers by recognizing their efforts and by expressing your appreciation. This will make your job more secure, enjoyable, and, most likely, be very valuable to you in your career path. After all, who would you rather promote, someone who has the respect and appreciation of those who work for him or with him or someone who does not?

"Fail to honor people they fail to honor you."

Lao Tzu

Who would you rather work for, someone who helps you in every way they can or someone who worries only about themselves? Who would you rather work with, someone who shares credit and shows appreciation to you or someone who hogs the credit and blames others for anything and everything that goes wrong? Who do you think your co-workers would rather work for or with?

You succeed by helping others get what they want. When you put everything else aside, people are what matters. People help people. People promote people. People and chemistry are what will often make the difference.

Help people and they will help you. You will never succeed without the help of others. Become known as someone who will go the extra mile. Stay late. Take on added responsibility, solve the difficult problems. Be known for these things and you will get ahead.

People tend to do more for people they like. They will go out of their way to help people they like. **They will work harder for people that appreciate their efforts.** They will go the extra mile for people they respect and appreciate. They will promote people they like over others if all else is even close to being equal.

This is not good, bad, or indifferent. It is the reality of the way things are. Look at your own actions toward others if you have any doubt of what I am telling you. It is simply human nature.

Chapter 18. Are you making your employer sick?

"All successful employers are stalking men who will do the unusual, men who think, men who attract attention by performing more than is expected of them."

Charles M. Schwab

If you are abusing the sick days your company gives you, you are a problem. A big problem. Your unjustified absenteeism reduces productivity. It hinders the company's ability to service their customers. It forces your co-workers to do your job and make up for your absence. It hurts quality control. It hurts your company in dozens of different ways. It costs a great deal of money. It hurts morale. It drives up overtime costs. It forces the company to carry more employees than they can justify.

This decreases profits or forces prices to increase which could result in lost sales. Either way, absenteeism lowers the company's profitability and this affects their ability to pay you better and provide greater benefits. But if you are abusing the company's sick days you shouldn't be thinking of lost profits or lower wages. **Maybe you should be thinking of how sick you will feel if you find yourself in the unemployment line. If you are abusing sick days this is where you belong.**

Do you know that statistics have shown that on average every employee will take 9 sick days per year? I know from personal experience that many so-called sick days are bogus. Sick days are one of the biggest areas of abuse among employees.

It has been projected that during 1994, every week over 4.5 million American workers were absent from their jobs at least one day. That's right 4.5 million lost days per week. This translates into over 1.8 billion lost hours per year to American companies.

Think about this. These are stunning totals.

If your company has 50 employees and each takes nine sick days, take a few minutes and figure out how much this lost 450 days of labor is costing the company. If your company has 50,000 employees and each averages 9 sick days per year the company has lost the equivalent of 450,000 work days.

The two primary things I have always looked for when I hire anyone at any level is attitude and attendance. If an employee has the right attitude, they can learn the job and do it well. No matter how well they do the job, they won't do me much good if they have poor attendance.

What is that you say? If you could save up sick days or get paid for those you did not use you would take fewer? I have heard this often. It is **a battle cry of mediocrity.** Think about that. Think about it some more.

This is a prime example of why this country is being driven to mediocrity. Is this not saying very clearly that you are staying out sick when you could be coming to work, that you are calling in sick when you are not, and simply that you are abusing the benefit your company has provided you?

My response to this often stated argument of mediocrity is very simple. Why should I pay you not to be out sick when I am already paying you to be at work? Isn't this paying for the same thing twice?

If you can manage to come to work more often if I pay you twice, then you can sure as heck come to work more often without any hardship if you want to keep your job.

Remember, every relationship is a two way street. If you are taking more than you are giving, you don't deserve to stay in the relationship. In this case, the job.

Sick days are provided to help you during the times you are sick or injured. They are something you should be thankful you have. They are not a benefit to be used whenever you feel you want a "free day".

They are not provided so you can use them as added free vacation time.

Derrick W. Welch

They have a purpose. The purpose is to make sure you are paid when you are unable to come to work.

If you use them for any other purpose, you are cheating your company and abusing a benefit provided to you. You are also making things much harder on your co-workers and hurting your company in hundreds of ways.

You are paid to be at work. Some seem to think that they are entitled to sick days. That if they don't use them somehow they are being cheated out of free days. To avoid this they make sure they use as many as they can. Or they demand payment for the ones they did not use, or in the cases of some unions or civil servants, demand they be allowed to save them up to be used later or cashed in.

In the city that I live we just had 3 policemen retire and get paid for hundreds of sick days they never used. This is a disgrace. These people were paid for being at work. They also expect to get paid extra for actually coming to work.

The average person works only 249 days a year, excluding holidays. If you have 3 weeks vacation a year, is the company not already paying you for 249 days when you are only at work 234 days? If you have 15 sick days a year and you use them all, the company is now paying you based on 249 working days a year when you are only on the job for 219 days. Do you see something wrong here?

Do you like paying for something you never received? Is this not the same thing you would be causing to happen to your employer? Is this not the same thing that happens when you ask for payment to be made when you do not use sick days? Does this seem right?

Does this seem like the mind-set of someone driven to excel? Driven to defy mediocrity? The mind-set of the person that thinks this way is the mind-set of mediocrity.

Chapter 19. You could be stealing from the company and not even know it.

"Rather fail with honor than succeed with fraud."

Sophocles

The United States Chamber of Commerce has conducted studies that indicate 75% of all employees have stolen at least once from their employer. Excluding the theft of time, they estimated that in 1994 alone employee theft cost U.S. businesses over $40 billion dollars. One insurance company has even stated that 1 out of 3 small businesses fail as a direct result of employee theft.

From taking home a few pens and pencils to "borrowing" materials from the company, these innocent and seemingly insignificant acts are theft. It might seem insignificant to you, but it is still wrong. It is no different than reaching into the petty cash box and taking money. The company paid for these materials, not you. It is company property. If you take it are you not taking someone else's property? Is this not theft?

"To see what is right and not do it, is want of courage, or of principle."

Confucius

Stealing time also makes you a thief. You are being paid to work a specific number of hours per day. When you steal time you are stealing money. You are being unfair to your co-workers. You are setting a bad example. You are hindering your company's ability to provide excellent customer service. You are hindering internal customer service. You are lowering productivity and you are lowering profitability. Stealing time is a big problem. It is not a minor issue. **It is a silent theft**. It is an invisible drain on productivity and profits.

You are hindering your company's ability to get the job done, product out, or service rendered, in the most productive and profitable manner possible. Your co-workers must work harder to make up for the time you are not working. Productivity is lowered so profits suffer or prices might go up. This could hurt sales which, in turn, could hurt profits. A cycle is created. A cycle of mediocrity.

"Waste of time is the most extravagant of all expenses."

Theophrastus

In fact, one of the biggest thefts an employee can make from an employer is the theft of time. Long breaks, extended lunches, personal phone calls on company time, standing around the time clock waiting for it to click to the punch out time, faking sick time, arriving late, and socializing during work time are just some of the many ways time is stolen from a company.

If you think I am overstating the problem and that a few minutes each day won't add up to much let me give you an example in dollars and cents to make my point more vivid. An employee making $12 per hour is being paid 20 cents per minute, not including payroll indexed costs. At 20 cents per minute even 5 minutes a day of wasted time is costing $1 per day. This is $5 per week or $260 per year.

Big deal you say? Well, then think about this. If 5 employees waste 5 minutes a day, this is costing your company $1,300 per year. If 50 employees waste even 5 minutes a day, it is costing your company $13,000 per year. If 500 employees waste 5 minutes a day, it is costing your company $130,000 per year. If 5,000 employees waste 5 minutes a day, this mere 5 minutes a day of wasted time will cost your company $1,300,000 per year. And if 50,000 employees waste just these few minutes each day, your company is effectively losing $13,000,000 per year. I assure you most of you waste a great deal more than 5 minutes per day. As you can see, it does not take long for small amounts of time to add up to serious money. **Don't be part of the problem. Defy mediocrity and become part of the solution.**

Chapter 20. Take your job seriously, but remember it is not life or death.

"Adversity causes some men to break; others to break records."

William A. Ward

In the worst case stress can kill you. It can make you sick. It can disrupt your ability to properly perform your job.

Stress will do you no good and a stressed out manager or employee cannot be effective and, as a result, will do your employer very little good.

Stress can cause you to make mistakes. Stress can cause you to lose focus. Stress can cause you to make the wrong decisions. It can cause you to make irrational and illogical decisions and take regrettable actions.

Stress can cause you to be reactive and defensive. It can make you lose your temper and react to people who do not deserve your wrath. It can cause irreparable harm in your work relationships and cause you to get a label you may never shake.

In short, nothing good will come from stress. But let me tell you something. Most stress is self-inflicted. You are putting the stress on yourself or letting others place too much stress on you. You are making major problems out of minor ones.

When you are under stress, try to put things in perspective and think clearly before you act or react. Most often you will find the level of stress you perceive to exist to really be far less.

The more stress you put yourself under the less effective your performance will be. A good example of this is a fighter. I once watched a fight between a superbly conditioned young fighter with tremendous skills and an older veteran.

Clearly the younger fighter was in better condition and had greater skills. But by the 6th round he was so tired he could barely stand up. The pressure and stress had gotten to him and he lost.

Unless he can learn to deal with it, he will never be the quality fighter he could and should be. Unless he learns to deal with stress, he will never reach the level of excellence he is clearly capable of. Instead, he will wallow in mediocrity.

Stress will make your enthusiasm drain away. Your disposition will be terrible. These factors will be reflected directly in your job performance and interaction with your co-workers, employees, or customers.

Learn to put stress in its place. Prioritize the jobs, problems, or tasks at hand and do each to the best of your ability based on the level of priority each requires. What more can you do? What more can you expect of yourself? What more can others expect of you?

"Things which matter most must never be at the mercy of things which matter least."

Goethe

The point is to do the most important things first. The things that must take priority. The things that will have the most impact. The things that will make the most bottom line impact. The things that are most pressing and will relieve the most pressure and, therefore, stress.

Let me give you a suggestion that I use to prioritize jobs and as a very simple and highly effective time management tool. I have never found a simpler or more effective way to prioritize work.

I keep a "to do" list using 3 x 5 index cards. I find these to be extremely effective. I can shift the most pressing or top priority task to the top of the list by simply shuffling the pile and once a task is done I can dispose of the card to reduce my pile.

The use of these cards in itself is a time saver since I am not constantly redoing a "to do" list. I simply toss out each card when the task is completed and add a new one as needed. I do not need to waste time every day creating a new list.

Never forget that most stress, like mediocrity, is self-inflicted.

Derrick W. Welch

Chapter 21. Defying mediocrity is a lot easier than you might think.

"The average person puts only 25% of his energy and ability into his work. The world takes off its hat to those who put in more than 50% of their capacity, and stands on its head for those few and far between souls who devote 100%."

Andrew Carnegie

A recent study by the Public Agenda Foundation, a private research organization, found that 44% of all employees surveyed admitted that they "exert no effort over the minimum".

With this in mind, let me ask you, how hard can it be to be a standout employee?

According to a report in Today's Office, a study of United States Personnel Directors from both large and medium companies indicated that "the average on-the-job performance of American workers is only fifty three percent of their total capacity".

Yes, you read that right, 53%. This means that 47% of the time the average American worker is engaged in non productive or non job-related activity. A nonproductive or non job related activity means a non-income producing activity. It means they are embracing mediocrity and not pursuing excellence.

In another study, a private research company in New York conducted a survey among employees to find out if they felt they gave their maximum effort at work each day. The results of this survey indicated that 77% of the employees surveyed, by their own admission, did not. Furthermore, nearly 50% indicated that they put forth no more than the minimum effort each day.

" It is more than probable that the average man could, with no injury to his health, increase his efficiency fifty percent. "

Walter Dill Scott

Finally, Business Week has reported that over the last 18 years factory productivity has gone up 51% but individual employee productivity has gone down 7%. This, despite the tremendous advances that have been made technologically during this time. **So, if you think you can't easily rise above mediocrity, think again.**

"Not doing more than average is what keeps the average down."

Wm. M. Winans

<u>Just by working a bit harder each day you will be far ahead of most others. Far ahead of mediocrity.</u>

As I have told you many times, it simply is not very difficult to defy mediocrity. It simply is not very difficult to become much better at what you do. It simply is not very difficult to exceed the expectations of others. It simply is not very difficult to dramatically increase your value to the company.

If you increase your value to the company, you will increase your earnings and be presented with more opportunities. Also remember the age of employment instability we live in. Which employee do you think will be kept when layoffs occur or will be considered for a promotion when an opening comes up, the employee who puts in no more than the minimum effort each day, the employee who puts in only 50% of the effort they could be putting in, or the employee who puts forth 100% effort every day?

Which will you be?

Chapter 22. The fear of failure.

"Timidity causes mistakes."

Jack Welch, CEO of General Electric

Perhaps the biggest mistake you can make is being afraid to make a mistake. What is the worst that can happen? In most cases it will be minor. Don't be afraid to say "I screwed up". "I was wrong". You might dent your ego and feel a bit embarrassed, but people will respect your candor and honesty and willingness to admit you are not infallible and that you can and do make mistakes. They will appreciate your willingness to accept responsibility. An unusual trait.

"Our doubts are our traitors, and make us lose the good we oft might win by fearing to attempt."

William Shakespeare

Who doesn't make mistakes? What is the worst that can happen in most cases? Your idea did not work? Your added efforts did not pay off as you had hoped?

So what? You may have gained invaluable lessons along the way. Failure can be the best teacher of all. Have you ever had the pleasure of watching a child try to walk for the first time?

They take a step and fall. Then one day they take two steps and fall. Then three steps and again they fall. Fall after fall. Failure after failure. But each failure is merely one more step on the path that leads to success. If children gave up after the first failure we would all be crawling around on our bellies.

Never forget that failing to succeed is not failure. The only failure is not trying at all.

Defy Mediocrity: <u>The</u> Employee's 90 Minute Guide To Excellence

"One who fears failure limits his activities. Failure is only the opportunity to begin again more intelligently."

Henry Ford

Every effort will not lead to success. In fact, most will not. Major league baseball players who fail 70% of the time become millionaires because they hit the ball safely a mere 30% of the time.

Thomas Edison failed to invent the light bulb over 11,000 times. Each time was merely one more step in his path to success.

"Do not be too timid or squeamish about your actions . All life is an experiment."

Ralph Waldo Emerson

Never be afraid to try, to stretch yourself, to suggest new ways of doing things or new ideas. <u>Too many people are so concerned with the possible consequences of making a mistake that they will pass an opportunity by rather than take a risk.</u>

They will stagnate rather than seek improvement. They will keep silent rather than speak up with an idea for improvement. If your ancestors were afraid of change, of challenge, of self-assessment, we might still be starting fires by banging two rocks together.

Don't get caught up in the trap of analysis paralysis. Don't analyze something so much that you never do anything. You never make a decision or take action. Inaction will very often be worse than the wrong action.

Most decisions or actions are not irreversible. You can make mistakes and correct most if needed.

Being known as someone not afraid to make a decision and take action and who is big enough to admit making mistakes and will take action to correct them is a reputation you should be proud to have.

"The majority of men meet with failure because of their lack of persistence in creating new plans to take the place of those which fail."

Napoleon Hill

Without some risk of failure or error nothing will ever get accomplished. Playing it safe will not get you or your company anywhere. This is like running on a treadmill. You go through a lot of motions but you never get anywhere. Remember, you can never get to second base if you never take your foot off first base. Few results, large or small, can be achieved without some risk, some price being paid.

One of the most common reasons for failure is that people give up when they suffer a defeat. Do you think the road to a successful job is defeat free? Does every NFL team score on every play? On every series of downs? Of course not.

They all suffer setbacks and defeats. In fact, far more defeats than successes. How those defeats are handled and what is learned from them is the key to success. Embrace defeat and failure for it is the surest path to the accomplishment of your objectives.

Fear holds most people back. Fear of failure. Fear of ridicule. Fear of risk. Most fears are only in your mind. Stand up and standout.

Fear is one shore that borders the sea of mediocrity. Defy it.

Chapter 23. Talk to me.

"When nothing seems to help I go and look at a stonecutter hammering away at his rock perhaps a hundred times without as much as a crack showing in it. Yet on the hundred and first blow it will split in two, and I know it was not that blow that did it - but all that had gone before."

Jacob Riis

One of the great failings of management today at all levels is the lack of positive reinforcement given to co-workers and employees. Most do not give, or do not have a clue as to how to give, positive reinforcement.

<u>If you are among this group do something about it. Start giving the people you work with and who work for you the verbal and visible recognition and appreciation they not only deserve, but need.</u>

Talk to your people. Tell them when things are done well. Tell them how they can get better. Tell them your expectations and help them meet them. People need feedback, direction, guidance, and appreciation. They will look for others to provide the reinforcement they need to validate their efforts and value. We all seek external validation.

If you work with or for someone who does not give you the appreciation, motivation, and feedback you need then don't wait to get it. Give it to yourself. Self-talk can be a great confidence builder. It can remind you of all the things you have done and can do.

It is mental conditioning just like exercise is physical conditioning.

"Men are born to succeed, not to fail."

Henry David Thoreau

Think of the many good things you have done. The difficult tasks you have faced and accomplished. The success you have had. The setbacks you have overcome.

Remind yourself that no one else in the world is just like you. No one thinks like you. No one looks just like you. No one that has come before you, or will come after you, is just like you. You are unique. Never forget this.

Put these thoughts and reminders down on paper and read them each day. Record them on a cassette and listen to them each day. Self-esteem and self-confidence are powerful tools. We need to feed our mind with positive reinforcement to build our self-confidence and self-esteem.

If we wait for others to provide the positive reinforcement we need, we may never get it.

We are all creatures of many frailties but most of us have much greater capabilities than our level of self-confidence and self-esteem lets us think. Use these self-talk tapes or written messages to boost your self-confidence and self-esteem.

You might feel strange doing it, but let me tell you it works and it works well. None of us hear enough good things about our performance and our ability. If others don't tell us, we will never hear it unless we tell ourselves.

Music can also be a great motivator. It can lift your spirits and improve your attitude and outlook. I don't know why. But I know it works.

It soothes the soul. It can give you confidence and enthusiasm. It can free you from the shackles of your mind. It will help you think clearer. It will help you think beyond the boundaries of your normal thought process by removing your problems and tedious thoughts from your conscious mind so thoughts and ideas can filter up from your subconscious mind.

Try it.

Chapter 24. Promises, promises.

"You can't build a reputation on what you're going to do."

Henry Ford

Always do what you say you are going to do. Your word is your bond. Whether you give it to a fellow employee, boss, or customer, never make a promise or commitment you cannot or will not keep.

You must always do what you say you are going to do. You must become known as an individual who follows through on what they say and on commitments they make. Others must know they can count on you. Others will make commitments based on your commitment. If you let them down they will be letting others down. It is a chain reaction. You are a key link in the chain.

"He who permits himself to tell a lie once finds it much easier to do it a second time."

Thomas Jefferson

Treat your word as a contract not to be broken. Contracts are the creation of lawyers, your word should be your bond.

If, for some unavoidable reason, you are unable to live up to a promise or commitment you made, make sure you tell all parties affected as soon as possible. They are counting on you and others are most likely counting on them. Your inability to live up to your commitment will affect the ability of others to live up to their commitment.

Think of it as the first domino in a line of dominos standing on end one after the other. When one falls it knocks all the others over. Give them some warning so they can compensate if possible and needed.

People must know they can count on you. Become a "can do" and "does it" person, not a "can't do" or doesn't do it" person. Which would you rather have working for you? Which type of person would you rather work with? Which type of person would you rather work for?

Which do you think your employer would rather have working for them? Which type of person do you feel they will look to advance fastest? Which type of person do you think will be noticed most? Counted on most? Compensated most? Respected most? Appreciated most?

In a world filled with mediocrity, people often say whatever they think you want to hear or whatever it takes to get rid of you. Don't you become one of them. Be the exception. Defy mediocrity.

Chapter 25. Free yourself from the shackles of your mind.

"Discovery (of a solution) consists of looking at the same thing as everyone else and thinking something different."

Albert Szent-Gyorgyi

Learn to think beyond the norm. Learn to think outside of the boundaries and the traditional reference points. We all have reference points. Reference points are merely the known options we have at our disposal to use in accomplishing something. When faced with a problem most of us consider those known options only.

"If everyone is thinking alike then someone isn't thinking."

George S. Patton

Options that reflect the way things have been done in the past. You must expand beyond these and develop new ways to accomplish the objectives of your job. This is how all progress is made. By not being satisfied with the known way of doing something you are forced to think beyond the boundaries and consider new ways to do the same thing.

"Watch your step when you immediately know the one way to do anything. Nine times out of ten, there are several better ways."

Wm. B. Given Jr.

From ways to save money to efforts for self-improvement, allow your mind to look beyond the boundaries. From a way to improve quality to improving productivity, look beyond the obvious, the tried and true, the traditional. Considering only the known options will never result in the improvements that are possible.

Good examples of this are overnight delivery services. Who ever thought we needed them? Fred Smith the founder of Federal Express did. Now we can't live without them. How about the fax machine. With phones, mail, and overnight delivery who ever thought we needed instant delivery? Now they are a way of business life for many companies.

Before these innovations came along if you needed to send something fast your only reference (known option) would have been to use the post office.

Another example of thinking beyond the boundaries is the home shopping club. With retail stores, personal shoppers, and direct mail shopping who knew we needed the ability to shop by phone from what amounts to a TV catalog?

But you do not need to create an industry or invent a new technology. Your small idea for doing things a new way may be equally important to your company. One idea can save tremendous amounts of money for your company and advance your career. Your one thought on how to improve productivity could make major improvements to the bottom line of your employer.

Your one idea on how to improve your product could dramatically improve quality or increase sales. Your one idea for sales to a new market could make an important impact. Your idea to reduce shipping costs matters. Your idea to speed up processing is important. Your idea for improved customer service counts. Your idea, no matter how small or large, can make a difference.

For example, one of the 1,000 cost control, expense reduction, and income producing ideas I give in my book "In Pursuit of Profits: How To At Least Double Your Profits Without Increasing Your Sales", is to re-use incoming boxes and cartons for outgoing shipments. I suggest that you use these boxes with a stamp or sticker indicating that as a responsible corporate citizen you are doing your part to help conserve the earth's resources by recycling boxes.

This way you are not perceived as a penny pinching company, but an environmentally sensitive company.

One small distributor used this one idea to save over $30,000 per year in packaging costs. At a 2.5% net profit ratio, this one small idea was equal to the net profits realized on gross sales of $1,200,000.

Another strategy I offer in that book is to use an inexpensive one color version of your corporate letterhead on a cheaper grade of bond paper for all secondary and internal correspondence. I suggest only using the multi-color, higher quality letterhead for corresponding with customers.

I know one large company that used this simple strategy to reduce letterhead and envelope costs by over $130,000 per year. Again, if this company's net profit was 2.5%, this bottom line savings of $130,000 per year was equal to the net profit on $5,200,000 of gross sales.

Minor ideas can, indeed, make a major impact.

In fact, I used the ideas and strategies in this book to increase the profits of my company over 450% in just 2 years!

"Towering genius disdains a beaten path. It seeks regions hitherto unexplored. It scorns to tread in the footsteps of any predecessor, however illustrious. It thirsts and burns for distinction."

Abraham Lincoln

All progress, no matter how small or how large, starts with someone thinking of a better way to do something, You are that someone.

Chapter 26. Don't let your ego get in the way of the objective.

"I not only used the brains I had, but all that I could borrow."

Woodrow Wilson

You don't know everything. Don't act like you do. Someone else will always know something you don't. Listen and learn.

"Personally, I'm always ready to learn, although I do not always like being taught."

Winston Churchill

Listen. As good as you may be at something and as knowledgeable or experienced as you might be, never forget that others can provide you valuable information. They may see something you do not. They may have a unique angle on a new way to do something, to improve quality, to increase production, for a new product, or a new market.

Sometimes being very good at what we do causes us to put on blinders. We think no one knows it better than us and, therefore, we do not even consider thoughts from others. We may not even know we are blocking these thoughts out by closing our minds.

Furthermore, an idea from someone else may cause us to modify a thought or idea and think in an entirely new way. There is always a better way. You do not know everything and never will. Neither do I nor will I.

We can, and should, listen. Listen and learn.

Chapter 27. Criticism. It can hurt, but it can also help.

"You can't let praise or criticism get to you. It is a weakness to get caught up in either one. Some criticism will be honest and some won't. Some praise you will deserve and some you won't. You have to take both in the same light."

John Wooden

Always listen to suggestions for improvement and what you might perceive as criticism.

What do you do when you are criticized? Do you react like a cat does when it sees a dog? Do you get defensive? Do you get mad? Do you think "the hell with them"? Do you blindly try to defend or justify your actions or inactions?

<u>Any fool can defend mistakes and most do.</u> Those that can admit their mistakes, correct them if possible, not make them again, learn from them, teach others not to make the same ones, and move on are the ones who will be the leaders. The ones who secure their jobs and open up the doors of advancement.

You will never be able to avoid criticism. In fact, I suggest you don't even try. Instead, when you are criticized, when you are second guessed, the first thing you should do is look within. Is the criticism or concern justified? Ask yourself if the point is valid. Ask yourself the questions.

Did you make a mistake? Were you wrong? Could you have done better? Was there another option you overlooked? Could you have handled the situation differently to get better results? Have you been guilty of whatever the person criticizing you claims?

Don't just dig your heels in and take a pig-headed stance. This gains you nothing but perhaps an enemy or a poor reputation.

Self-assessment is a very difficult thing to do. It is very hard to admit you made a mistake or that you could have done something better or differently with better results. But if you could have, admit it, learn from it, correct or adjust things if possible, and move on.

Learn any lesson there is to learn and move on. You can't be moving forward if you are still in the past.

Few things are more unproductive and damaging to your self-esteem than dwelling on past mistakes, failures, missed opportunities, or resentment for criticism, justified or not.

If the criticism is not justified forget it. Don't get caught up in it. Don't waste time fuming over it. Don't go around mouthing off to others about how unfair it was or how the person criticizing you was wrong. It is nonproductive and can seriously damage your attitude.

The employee in pursuit of excellence will learn any lesson to be learned and move forward. The mediocre employee will dwell on the situation and, by doing so, will put even more roadblocks in front of himself. Self-inflicted roadblocks.

Which will you be?

Chapter 28.   Don't let the number of pieces get in the way of finishing the puzzle.

"Life is frittered away by details. Simplify. Simplify."

Henry David Thoreau

Many tasks you are faced with on the job each day can seem overwhelming. They may seem so large and complex that you don't even know how to begin. They may seem so all encompassing you may immediately start to look for excuses not to begin them or why you should not do them.

You may begin building a justification for failure without even realizing it. You may waste valuable time by going around informing everyone of the tremendous task you are faced with. These and similar actions will serve only to ensure that the project or task will never be completed. You have already begun to mentally give up. <u>Mediocrity has won the battle before you even enter the war.</u>

"Nothing is particularly hard if you divide it into small jobs."

Henry Ford

The key to dealing with complexity is to break it down into simple steps. Break a big job down into a series of small jobs. If you had a choice between simple or complex which would you choose?

Always proceed with the goal of simplicity. Most things are simply not as complex or daunting as they may appear at first. Don't make them out to be more complex than they are. Do not allow them to become more complex than they must be. The completion of a series of small tasks or steps results in the completion of the overall task.

It really is that simple. Don't compound the issue.

Derrick W. Welch

Chapter 29. Oh great! Another damn problem.

"Fix the problem, not the blame"

old Japanese saying

Problems. Most employees hate them. Most employees try to ignore them, hoping they will go away. They pretend not to be aware of them. Some try to pass them off to others. Most see them as an inconvenience or intrusion into whatever they think their job is. Most will blame others for them. Blaming someone else will never solve the problem. It merely creates another one.

"In the middle of difficulty lies opportunity."

Albert Einstein

A rare few embrace problems and see them as an opportunity to find a resolution that will benefit the company in some manner and improve their skills and capabilities. These rare few understand that problems should not be ignored. These rare few understand that they can represent opportunity. An opportunity to rise above mediocrity. To rise above others.

These rare few understand that without problems they might not be needed. These rare few understand that the acceptance and resolution of problems is one more way to defy mediocrity. These rare few consider a problem a challenge. **These are the employees who are defying mediocrity. The employees who are pursuing excellence.**

If your company didn't have problems, you might not be needed. Machines or robots could do most tasks if problem solving was not part of the job. Do you think that it is not your job to address problems? Do you think problems are someone else's responsibility? Do you think that problems will go away if you ignore them?

If so, allow me to point a few things out to you. First of all, problems will not go away. They will get worse and may even become irreparable if they are not addressed.

Secondly, passing a problem off to someone else may get rid of the problem, but it represents terrible internal customer service and will do nothing to advance your career, to improve your skills, to endear you to your co-workers and customers, or to increase your self-esteem. Hiding never will.

Do you want others passing off problems to you? If it were your company, would you want your employees doing all they could to ignore or pass off problems?

"There are three kinds of people;
Those who make things happen,
those who watch things happen,
and those who don't know what the hell is happening."
Dr. Robert Anthony

Which are you?

Derrick W. Welch

Chapter 30. Integrity. Initiative. Attitude. Pride. The pillars of excellence. The four main weapons you must have in your battle to defy and defeat mediocrity.

Integrity

"It's not hard to make decisions when you know what your values are."

Roy Disney

There is a line from the old TV show Dallas that I have always remembered. It was spoken by the show's main villain, J.R. Ewing, who was played by Larry Hagman. After he had just finished destroying someone in a business deal and stealing his adversary's wife he was asked "How can you do that? How can you live with yourself?" J.R. turned and responded "Once you lose your integrity, the rest is easy".

It all starts with integrity. Integrity is about doing the best you can. Integrity is about honesty. Integrity is about doing what is right. You always know what is right or wrong.

Initiative

"Even in the most opportune times doors do not open themselves. The initiative must always be taken by those outside the doors."

Bess Myerson

Initiative is about being determined to make a difference. It is about doing something before you are asked to. It is about developing ideas and thinking about how to do your job better. It is about going the extra step. It is about seeing something that needs to be done and doing it whether or not it is "your job". Initiative is about seeing a way to help someone and helping them without worrying about getting credit for it. Initiative is about doing the most with what you have to work with instead of finding reasons why you can't.

Initiative is about making the job of others easier and not worrying about making your own job easier. Initiative is about fixing the problem and not trying to figure out how to affix the blame.

Initiative is about showing me and not telling me. Initiative is about knowing that if you can do better, "good enough" will never be. Initiative is about producing results, not creating excuses. <u>Initiative is about not hiding behind union rules or civil servant protective policies to avoid doing the best you can.</u>

Attitude

"Attitude. The magic word. With the right one you can accomplish anything. Without it you will wallow in mediocrity."

Derrick W. Welch

It all starts with attitude. An attitude of trying to become better at what you do. An attitude of doing the best you can every minute of every day. An attitude of setting an example for others. An attitude of self-assessment reflected in a constant quest for being a better, more capable person.

I am not talking about transcendental meditation, self visualization, positive thinking, I'm O.K., you're O.K.. I am talking about attitude. One of the most powerful words in the English language.

An attitude of helpfulness. An attitude of putting the responsibility of the job ahead of your personal agenda. An attitude of making the product better by doing your job better. An attitude of providing superior external customer service by providing superior internal service. An attitude of "it is never good enough" instead of "that's good enough". An attitude of pride in what you do and how well you do it.

Derrick W. Welch

Pride

"If a man is called to be a streetsweeper, he should sweep streets even as Michelangelo painted, or Beethoven composed music, or Shakespeare wrote poetry. He should sweep streets so well that all the hosts of heaven and earth will pause to say, here lived a great streetsweeper who did his job well."

Martin Luther King Jr.

Pride. It always comes down to pride. Pride in what you do and how well you do it. Pride in doing the best job you can, no matter who is or is not watching you, no matter how seemingly mundane or insignificant the task is. Pride in constantly striving to be better at what you do. <u>Pride in knowing that how much you did will never outweigh how well you did it.</u>

Think about this. You spend over half of your life at work, getting to work, coming from work or thinking about work. Don't you think you should take pride in your work? Don't you think a subpar work performance will affect you outside of the office? Lower your self-esteem? An attitude of doing your best every day in every way has to carry over in a positive manner to all other areas of your life.

How could it not? You are building a mind-set of excellence or mediocrity based on your job performance. Which are you building? A mind-set that carries over into every other area of your life whether you want to admit it or not.

Never forget that your work is a reflection of yourself. How do you look to others? To yourself? **Take pride in what you do and how well you do it!**

Chapter 31.   Mediocrity does, indeed, love company. Dare to be different.

"The scarcest resources in any organization are performing people."

Harvard Business Review Jan. - Feb. 1995

One cause of mediocrity is pressure from other employees. Other employees who try to get you to join them in doing little more than you have to do to keep your job. They worry that if you do more they will look poor by comparison. If you strive to improve quality, they will look bad by comparison.

If you develop ideas for improvements, or undertake efforts to improve yourself and your capabilities, they may resent you as they will pale by comparison. This is a disgrace and a prime symptom of mediocrity.

You must ignore these people and rise above them. **What do you care about making them look bad?** They are the ones making themselves look bad. Are you going to let them make you look bad by allowing them to keep you down with them?

That is their problem. Let them start worrying about how to do the job as well as you do it and before you know it the pressure will be on those who are not doing the job as well as they can. The end result will be that everyone will be better and the company will be better for it.

Don't be afraid to make waves if it can help you do a better job or your company become a better company. Because you are surrounded by mediocrity, you will often be confronted with an attitude of complacency and of doing things the way they have always been done.

Your suggestions for change or improvement, and, indeed, your own efforts to improve, will not always be greeted with the enthusiasm and recognition they deserve. Don't let this stand in your way.

Speak up if you need to. Let others know of your idea. If it can help the company in some manner it must be made known and given a chance. Don't let someone else cause you to abandon an idea for improvement.

Don't let fear hold you back. Fear of ridicule from your co-workers. Fear of failure. Fear of resentment from others in the company who thrive in a mixture of complacency and mediocrity.

This is all bull! Each of these fears stems from what others may think of you. Those trying to do better will always be a target for those who coast through life and do no more than they absolutely have to.

Think about this. These are the people at the root of your fears. These creatures of complacency. These marathon swimmers in a sea of mediocrity. Are these the people whose standards you are afraid of?

Wake up and smarten up. Let your actions put you so far above these people that you can't even see them anymore. Because so many are mediocre, it is simply not very difficult to rise above them and separate yourself from this group.

These people will never have initiative or drive. They will try to hold you down. Like a swimmer trying to cross the English channel with weights on his legs they want you to drown in the sea of mediocrity they flourish in.

"I would sooner fail than not be among the greatest."

John Keats

Forget these people. They are mediocrity. Defy them by doing the best you can each and every day. Defy them by constantly seeking to become better and more capable. Defy them.

You can't control what someone else does, but you can control what you do. You must strive to do the best you can regardless of what others do. Remember, the vast majority embrace mediocrity.

They do nothing more than the absolute bare minimum and, even, then mediocrity would be a step up for many of these people.

Do your best and worry about yourself, not them. Don't take the attitude that you will if they do or you won't because they don't. This will drive you to mediocrity and you will be allowing other people's inactions or actions to determine your performance.

This must always be unacceptable.

Mediocrity loves company. Have the guts to rise above it.

Chapter 32. Stay above the fray.

"All unhappiness is caused by comparison."

Dr. Robert Anthony

Stop worrying about everyone else and start taking care of your own responsibilities. Stop worrying about what other people make or who got this or that. Stop worrying about who is doing this or that. Stop being jealous. Stop spreading rumors. Stop asking about things that do not concern you. Stop gossiping. It hurts your reputation. It hinders productivity. It often results in unfairly hurting others. <u>Tearing someone else down will never lift you up</u>.

"Nothing so needs reforming as other people's habits."

Mark Twain

Are you so perfect that you have time to worry about the faults or successes of others? Is your job being done so well that there is no room for improvement and you can waste time worrying and complaining about others?

Don't get involved in petty office politics, gossip, rumors, and personality conflicts. They are unproductive, they will hurt your career, they help no one. By even talking about them you are part of the problem. Your goal should always be to be part of the solution, not part of the problem. Do not get involved or you will be perpetuating the problem.

Stop worrying about others and, instead, focus on your own responsibilities and efforts. Forget the politics. The time you spend being jealous or resentful of others can never be recovered and will do nothing to advance you.

Defy Mediocrity: <u>The</u> Employee's 90 Minute Guide To Excellence

If you spend all your time talking negatively, you will have no time to act positively. Pointing out the problems and shortcomings of others will never result in your own self-improvement. How could it?

> *Sign on company bulletin board: "This firm requires no physical-fitness program. Everyone gets enough exercise jumping to conclusions, flying off the handle, running down the boss, flogging dead horses, knifing friends in the back, dodging responsibility and pushing their luck.".*

> *A story from Financial Times as reprinted in the April 1995 Readers Digest.*

Ride the horse, but don't shovel the manure. All too many people wallow in manure. They make major problems out of minor issues. They grasp at the smallest detail and focus in on it like a laser beam.

Life is too short. You simply do not have enough time to waste one minute on petty personality differences, office politics, envy, and water cooler gossip. Stay above the fray. Don't you have enough to worry about?

Chapter 33.   Commitment.

"The secret of success is consistency to purpose."

Benjamin Disraeli

The late great Earl Nightingale used to tell a story about a patron at a piano recital. The woman playing the piano was extraordinary. She enthralled the audience. After her performance the patron came up to her and complimented her on her skills. She told the pianist that she would love to be able to play as well as she could.

The pianist shocked her by responding "No, you wouldn't". The patron, taken aback, responded "Yes, yes I would love to play as well as you can". The pianist looked the patron in the eye and replied "No, no you wouldn't. You say you would, but you wouldn't. If you really would like to play as well as I do, you could. But you really don't want to or else you would have put in the 10 hours of practice a day for the last 18 years that I have.".

The pianist was talking about the difference between wishing and wanting and the commitment needed to reach the level one aspires to. The reality of it was that the patron was not willing to put forth the effort and the commitment needed to become as good as the pianist.

Are you willing to make the commitment and put forth the effort and make the sacrifices needed to become as good as you can be? To reach the level you aspire to?

Words have meaning. Few have a stronger meaning than commitment. Most people have no idea what the word really means. They may talk about it and may even claim to be committed, but it is very doubtful they are.

*"Nothing worthwhile ever happens quickly and easily. You achieve
only as you are determined to achieve .... and as you keep at it until
you have achieved. "*

Robert H. Laver

If you want to become better at what you do, you can. If you aspire to
higher levels of responsibility, you can reach them. If you want to earn
more, you can. All you need to do is commit to improving yourself so
you have the capability to accomplish what you seek. Stop wishing and
wanting. Stop whining and hoping. Start doing something about it.

There is a young woman who works for me named Larissa Towns. She
works as both a receptionist and as an order entry person. She knows
she has more capabilities than these jobs require. She knows she wants
more out of her career than this. She also knows that she does not have
the skills and experience to move above this level.

She is not whining about not getting the chance to advance. She does
not complain about others getting ahead faster than she is. She does not
stew in a pool of self-pity. Instead, she realizes that she must become
better and more capable. She knows she must increase her value to the
company if she wishes to move ahead.

So, at the age of 23 she decided to go to night school to gain the skills
she needed to move to the level that she seeks.

She has no illusions about the company owing her anything. She also
knows that by gaining more education and experience she will be
offered the opportunity she seeks. She knows that she must be ready
and capable to take advantage of any opportunity that presents itself.

To make sure she is, she goes to class 4 hours a night, three nights a
week, while working full-time. When many other woman her age are
out socializing and living life, she is preparing for the future.

She is committed to developing the skills and talents she needs to reach
her goals. She is willing to make the sacrifices needed to reach the level
she seeks.

She is defying mediocrity. She knows that a key to overcoming mediocrity is commitment. Commitment to becoming better at what she does and can do, both short and long term.

Let me tell you about a man I recently had the pleasure of meeting. His name is Carroll Cross and he is the CEO of his own company. What is so special about Mr. Cross? Well, for starters he holds over 15 patents and owns three other companies. Impressive to be sure, but this is not the point of my story.

Mr. Cross contacted me to see if I could help him plan for the future. He wanted to accomplish a number of things with his company and he felt he needed outside talent to help him reach his long term goals for the company. He wanted to lay a foundation for the future.

Mr. Cross happens to be 91 years old. Yes, you read that right. Mr. Cross is 91 years old. He has a 61 year old son. He works 8 hours a day, four and a half days a week. He is not a figurehead hanging on to a title. He is the first and last word in everything his company does. At the age of 91, Mr. Cross was thinking about the future and what he needed to do today to reach his goals tomorrow.

Most people would have been retired 20 or 30 years before. Not Mr. Cross. He is committed to doing what is needed to get where he wants to go.

Are you? Are you willing to take responsibility for your future and improve your skills so that you can improve your value to your company? Are you willing to stop whining about what you don't have and start improving the way you do things and increasing your capabilities so that your company can help you achieve what you seek in your career?

Are you willing to make the sacrifices needed to defy mediocrity and pursue the excellence that you are capable of? It won't happen by itself. Wishing and wanting will get you nowhere. Commitment will.

Chapter 34. Procrastination. One of mediocrity's best friends.

"Knowing is not enough, we must apply. Willing is not enough, we must do."

Goethe

I must confess that I will never understand those who procrastinate. I cannot understand how you can put something off that should be done. I will never understand how you can agree to do something and not do it or at least not until you have been reminded of it over and over again.

I will not coddle those of you who are procrastinators. I don't give a hoot what the psychologists and psychiatrists of the world dole out as excuses or justification for those who procrastinate. These well-meaning professionals have a tendency to give anyone and everyone an excuse for their failings. <u>My goal is to take those excuses away. To remove those self-serving justifications that so many hold onto as crutches to lend credibility to what often are self-inflicted inadequacies.</u>

Overcoming procrastination takes the same effort it takes to overcome any other bad habit in life. It takes the self-assessment to recognize the problem, a determination to eliminate the weakness and a commitment to getting it done.

If you are a procrastinator, you know that putting off things that need to be done only makes things worse. It can cost you customers. It can cost you promotions. It can cause serious morale problems. It can turn a simple task into a major problem. It can cost you your job. It is inexcusable!

"The way to do things is to begin."

Horace Greley

I see fewer things that are easier to overcome than the habit of procrastination. Don't think about things you need to do or should do.

Do them. The more you think about something the longer you delay doing something about it. The more you think about an unpleasant task the more reasons you will come up with not to do it or to delay doing it even longer.

If it must be done or needs to be done, do it. Thinking about it and planning for it will do nothing but make the task seem that much more difficult, thereby feeding your fear of doing the task.

If you have a difficult task to begin, start to work on it. If you must make an unpleasant phone call, pick up the phone and make it. If you know you need to reorder supplies but keep putting it off, get out your order form and order them. If you have a letter to write, write it.

If the equipment you are working with must be cleaned each week then clean it each week. Putting it off will merely make it much more difficult to clean later and could damage the machine. If the machine breaks down it will delay production, disrupt your customer service, cost money, and could otherwise severely hurt the company.

If you have an idea for improvement try it. Ideas without action are useless.

"In any moment of decision the best thing you can do is the right thing, the next best thing is the wrong thing, and the worst thing you can do is nothing."

Theodore Roosevelt

Medlocrity loves procrastinators Their actions or inactions, spill over into so many other areas of the company's operations and drag so many others into the circle of mediocrity, that procrastinators are one of mediocrity's great allies.

Defy mediocrity by defeating procrastination.

Chapter 35. Hey management, listen up.

"What we see depends mainly on what we look for."

John Lubbock

In psychology there is a term called the "Pygmalion effect". It refers to setting expectations for people to live up to. The theory is that if you treat people as though they are worthy of your expectations for them, they will seek to live up to your expectations of them. If you know I think you are good, it is very likely that you will work very hard to prove me right and live up to my expectations of you.

All too often management will not set expectations for their people to live up to. Instead, they develop a perception, right or wrong, of the capabilities of the individuals that work for them. They don't try to develop people. They make a decision of an employee's capabilities based on their perception of what that person is capable of. A perception that is often wrong.

My perception is my reality. So is yours. We must open our eyes and ears to other ideas and possibilities. Because we think it is, does not mean it is or must be.

Carl Sandburg made this point in a story in one of his books about folks from the east moving out west back around the turn of the century. He told the story about a farmer standing on the edge of his property on a hot and dusty day. A family rode up to him on their way out West in a creaking, dirt covered old wagon pulled by two tired looking horses.

The family asked the farmer what the people in the next town were like. The farmer responded by asking the family what the people were like in the town they came from. The family replied that most of the people from the town back home were not very friendly and not very honest.

The farmer then advised them that he suspected the people in the next town were pretty much like those people back home. The family shook their head in disappointment and continued on their journey.

A short time later another family happened by and stopped and asked the farmer what the people in the next town were like. The farmer once again responded by asking them what the people back home were like. The family replied by telling the farmer that the people back home were a friendly group of hard-working honest people. The farmer then told the family that he reckoned that they would find the same type of people in the town up ahead.

You see, people's perceptions are their reality. Perceptions can, for better or worse, become self-fulfilling prophecies. We act according to our perception. Acting according to our perception can make the perception we hold, again, good or bad, become a reality.

But, as a manager, you can help mold and modify those perceptions. If you, as a manager, think one of your people is not very talented or capable, then your actions and expectations will convey this and this will become your employee's perception of himself.

If, on the other hand, you feel, or act as though you feel, your employee is very talented and capable, your actions and expectations of him will reflect this and most likely he will strive to live up to your faith in him. This works. I know firsthand.

I have had great success in converting mediocre employees into excellent employees simply by being able to improve their perception of themselves by giving them expectations to live up to and letting them know I had tremendous faith in them.

No, it won't always work. But yes, many times it will and the little effort required is well worth it.

Try to set expectations for others to live up to. Telling someone you know they can do this or reach that objective is far more powerful and effective than telling someone they must do this or accomplish that.

You are setting expectations for them to strive for. Expectations they will want to meet out of pride and not fear. Give them something to live up to. Let them know you are counting on them and that you have faith in them. They won't want to let you down. Let them know how important their effort and input is.

Another problem created by incorrect perceptions is that very often good people have to change jobs to get ahead. The problem is that they are perceived **by management** as having one set of capabilities. Of having limitations that they may not even have. Because of this they are not given a chance to accomplish more. To be more involved. To be heard and make a greater impact.

As a result, they often have to change companies to move ahead. Many go to companies who can see their potential and who are not blinded by preconceived notions regarding their capabilities or limitations that may not even be remotely accurate. Others will strike out and start their own business and the company may find not only have they lost an excellent employee, but now they have a new competitor. A lot of top talent is lost this way. Don't you be guilty of this. Don't let your perception pigeonhole your people.

Don't force them to leave your company. Think of the time, effort, and cost of training them. Think of the investment you have in each employee. Think of the time, cost, and risk you will be faced with when you have to hire a replacement.

Your people are much more capable than you probably give them credit for. Start seeing their potential and start helping them develop it. Don't let <u>your</u> perception of their capabilities and limitations blind you to the reality of their potential.

Derrick W. Welch

Chapter 36.   The grass is often greenest in your own yard.

"Opportunity is missed by most people because it is dressed up in overalls and looks like work."

Thomas Edison

Dr. Russell Conwell, the founder of Temple University, used to tell a story about a man who owned a farm in Africa.   According to Dr. Conwell, the man owned acres of farmland. He owned this farm around the time that diamonds were being discovered throughout the continent. He got diamond fever, sold his farm, and spent the rest of his life looking for diamonds. Diamonds that he never found.

While the former farmer wasted his life looking for diamonds throughout the African continent the man who had bought his farm went about his work every day. One day while crossing a stream on his farm he saw a sparkling stone on the bottom of the creek bed. He picked up the stone and brought it back to the farm where it sat on his mantle as an ornament.

One day, months later, a geologist happened to be visiting the farmer. When he saw the stone he asked the farmer if he knew what the stone was. The farmer told the geologist that is was merely a block of crystal and that his creek bed was littered with such stones, although most were much smaller.

As you might expect, the farmer had no idea he had the largest diamond ever discovered sitting on his fireplace mantle. The farmer owned one of the richest diamonds finds in history. The man who had owned the farm and sought his fame and fortune elsewhere died a poor man.

The moral of this story is that the opportunity you are seeking may be best found right at the company you are working for now. It is up to you to develop the opportunity.

It is up to you to improve yourself so that you will be given the opportunity. It is up to you to improve your value to the company so the door of opportunity will open for you. You must earn the opportunity. It will not, and should not, just be given to you because you want it or think you deserve it.

If, at first, it appears that the opportunity you are seeking is not with your company, look around. The opportunity you seek may be with the company after all, it may merely be in another department or division within the company.

It is up to you to determine what the opportunity is that you are seeking and to develop the skills and capabilities you need to reach your objectives.

Things will often look greener elsewhere when you are looking for the easiest path to the door of opportunity you are seeking. But very often the best opportunity is right where you are now. You may simply not be seeing it because you are too busy looking elsewhere for the easier path.

The easier path that may exist only in your mind.

Chapter 37. There is a problem.

"Don't find a fault. Find a remedy."

Henry Ford

Pointing out problems is easy. Anybody can do it and most do. Defy mediocrity by developing solutions.

If you bring up problems, make sure you are also developing and offering solutions. Problems are easy to find. Bitching and moaning is easy. It takes no intelligence. It takes little effort. It accomplishes nothing but making others dread seeing you coming. It makes your boss wish he or she never hired you.

How favorable would you view a boss, employee, or co-worker who did nothing but whine, complain, and bring problems to your attention all day? As someone who deals with far too many people like this each day, I can assure you that you would not be very favorably inclined toward these people.

You would much prefer people who solve problems, people who stop a problem from ever reaching your desk, and people who offer solutions to problems along with the presentation of the problem. These are the types of people that management seeks.

Stop whining about problems and do something about them. Has whining about anything solved any problem you have ever had since you were older than 2 or 3? Has it ever produced a solution? You are wasting valuable time and resources.

No one, and I mean no one, wants to deal with an employee who points out every problem over and over without ever offering any suggestions for resolution. If you want to defy mediocrity start solving problems. You are far better off being known as a problem solver than you are being known as a whiner and complainer. You were hired to solve problems, not become one by pointing out every problem that you can find.

Stop dwelling on the problems and start focusing on the solutions. A good example is weekly meetings with various people in the company. All time is spent talking about problems. The problems never seem to end. Constant review of them severely hurts morale. It makes them seem larger than they are. They can appear overwhelming. Spending all your time talking about your problems also takes away from the time you could, and should be using to find solutions to those problems.

"Nothing will ever be attempted if all possible objections must first be overcome."

J.R. Simplot

Don't be afraid to try things and take a risk in your quest to solve the problem. Speak up with your ideas for a resolution. If you analyze the problem looking for the perfect, risk free, guaranteed solution you will never even attempt to find a solution. You will never find it.

Remember, Edison failed over 11,000 times before he created a light bulb that worked. If he had waited to find the perfect solution to his problem, or had spent all his time speaking of his problems and failed attempts, we might all be living in the dark.

"A failed attempt is not a failure. It is a teacher. "

Derrick W. Welch

Failure merely teaches you what won't work. It may teach you what might work or point the way to other ideas and possible solutions. It may have taught you that you have found part of the answer.

Identifying problems is a trademark of mediocrity. Finding resolutions to the problem and thereby eliminating the problem is yet one more way mediocrity is defeated and excellence is embraced.

Chapter 38. Why were you hired anyway? What is your real job?

"Profit is a must. There can be no security for any employee in any business that doesn't make money. There can be no growth for that business. There can be no opportunity for the individual to achieve his personal ambitions unless his company makes money."

Duncan C. Menzies

Understand from day one and every day after that, that you are on staff to produce profits, not products or services. Products and services are merely the vehicles used to accomplish the goal of profits. Anything that is undertaken that does not directly, or indirectly, produce profits should be questioned. Anything that has the potential to increase profits should be suggested and, if possible, attempted.

The more you can impact the bottom line of your employer, the more valuable you will be. The most important resource in any company is its people. They cannot succeed without your maximum effort. This is why you were hired. The company felt you had the skills and talent to help them accomplish their objective. You are a piece of the overall puzzle. People often forget about this.

Think before you act and ask the questions. Don't be a robot. Think about what you are doing and why. Think about how you can do it better and help others do the same. Think about how you can improve quality. Think about how you can improve productivity. Think about how you can cut costs without sacrificing quality.

Always remember your real value to the company lies in your ability to help them increase profits. Think before you act and act accordingly.

Chapter 39. The domino effect.

"It is not only what we do, but also what we do not do, for which we are accountable."

Moliere

Did you ever play dominos as a child? If you did, you know that one of the most enjoyable things to do with those spotted wooden blocks was not to play the game of dominos, but to stand them up on their ends, one after another, and then to knock the first one over. When you knocked the first one over it in turn fell on the second one, which, in turn, fell on the third one, which, in turn, fell on the fourth one, and this sequence continued until the last domino in line fell over.

The primary action you took was to knock over the first block. The secondary result was that you knocked all the others over as well. Your action of knocking over one caused a series of secondary actions. **I call this the domino effect.**

It is the same way in life. Every action you take in life produces a number of secondary results beyond the primary result you see. In every area of life this is true. If your actions are positive, you will realize many positive secondary benefits as a direct or indirect result of your primary action. The same thing is true on the job and the same thing is true for inaction.

For example, if you are a manager and you have an employee who comes in late every day, his actions will cause a reaction on your part. If your primary action is to take no action, the primary result will be that the problem will continue.

The secondary results are that you may have a morale problem among other employees who resent the fact that this employee is allowed to come in late all the time.

You will have a problem with your productivity since this person cannot be counted on. You may face a discrimination suit if you discipline another employee for the same attendance problems when you did nothing about the problem employee. You see your inactions also produce many results beyond the primary one.

Now, if you had taken action against this employee and your primary action was to terminate him, you have also caused a number of secondary results. You now may need to hire a new employee or, at the very least, reassign his job duties. You may suffer a temporary reduction in productivity. You may face higher unemployment rates as this employee may file for unemployment and get it despite your objections. You may see improved attendance as you have now sent a message to other employees. You see the effects of your primary actions ripple out well beyond the primary and most visible result. **A domino effect is created.**

Everything you do, or do not do, has an effect on someone or something else. If your productivity goes up, more product is pushed through and operational costs are lowered. This means increased profits. Increased profits may mean your company can pay you more or provide you with better benefits. It may mean your company can sell its goods and services for lower prices thereby increasing sales and creating a self-perpetuating cycle of lower costs due to economies of scale and increased profits.

If you improve quality you will produce fewer unacceptable products or services. This will reduce costs and improve productivity since redos are lowered. It could also result in an improved perception among your customers regarding the quality of your company's products and services. This could lead to an ability to charge higher prices due to the customer's perceived value of your products and services being higher. This, again, can lead to increased profitability and increased market share.

Increased profitability can allow your company to spend more on developing new products and opening new markets. This could lead to even higher profits which could lead to higher wages, improved working conditions, and better benefits.

Your efforts to increase quantity and quality will make your co-worker's jobs much easier. This will result in improved relations between you and your co-workers as well as between your department and other departments. This improves morale and increases respect between you and those you work with and for.

Compare this to the domino effect created when you stay out sick when you could have worked. Or when you constantly come in late or do shoddy work. What do you think will happen?

Let me give you a brief overview of the negative side of the domino effect. Your co-workers will resent you and will not support your efforts or aspirations in any way. Your boss might start thinking of ways to replace you, not to promote you.

The costs associated with your efforts will increase and this will cause profits to decrease. In the extreme case sales could decrease due to higher prices needed to restore profits and sales could fall. This could result in layoffs that could affect you and your co-workers.

If your company absorbs the higher costs instead of increasing prices to compensate for your poor efforts, this will result in lower profits which means lower, or perhaps even no, raises. It could mean employment cutbacks and wage freezes.

It could hinder your company's ability to develop new products and services as well as open new markets or expand existing markets. This would cost them market share.

The cycle of positive effects or negative effects resulting from your actions or inactions is far-reaching. Never underestimate the effect your actions have.

Let me give you another example. Think about what happens when a salesperson turns an order in that is not clearly written up and does not have complete processing instructions.

When the order comes in for processing a number of things could happen, all of which demonstrate a negative domino effect.

Derrick W. Welch

First, the order entry people can reject the order and send it back to the salesperson for clarification. This delays processing of the order which negatively affects customer service. It also costs money since time had to be taken to review the order, decide to return it, actually return it, and then it must be redone and resubmitted by the salesperson.

Another option would be for the home office folks to call the salesperson and seek clarification. This takes time and time costs money. Furthermore, in both of these cases the customer may need to be contacted again to get the needed information. This could shake the customer's confidence in both the company and the salesperson.

Another option would be for the home office to contact the customer to secure the needed clarification. The negative effects that I pointed out above apply here as well.

Perhaps the home office guesses at what the missing or unclear information is and processes the order based on that. When they do this, they are perpetuating the negative side of the domino effect. They may assume wrong and process the order incorrectly. This would mean they have wasted time and money to deliver an incorrect product. The customer will refuse to pay for the product and could cancel the original order. Even if they do not cancel the order it now must be redone, thereby costing the company money and lost productivity.

These are just some of the many different negative things that can happen all as a result of the salesperson not doing his or her job properly. The domino effect works both ways.

Yes, many times the secondary results of your positive primary action will be small and the results apparently not very significant. **But this is what defying mediocrity is all about.** You are realizing a primary gain and, by doing so, you are enjoying many secondary benefits that improve you and your company in many other ways.

"In a balanced organization, working toward a common objective, there is success."

T.L. Scrutton

Defy Mediocrity: <u>The</u> Employee's 90 Minute Guide To Excellence

If you and all your co-workers embrace a program of ongoing improvement, you are embracing a way of doing business that extends well beyond simply saving money and increasing profits. You are creating a focus for your company. You are creating an objective for every single person in your company. You are creating a culture for your organization. You are creating an internal mission statement that will guide the actions of all who are in your organization. You are instituting an evolutionary program designed to embark on a never-ending journey of improvement.

You are seeking to improve every area of your operation. From how you produce and deliver products and services to how you purchase and inventory products. From how you sell to how you service, you are constantly seeking ways to do it better, faster, and at a lower cost. You have a common goal with your company.

You are bringing individual objectives in line with corporate objectives. If you follow the advice I am giving you in this book, you will see stunning improvements in your morale and the morale of your co-workers. This will lead to improved productivity, improved attendance, better service, increased quality, and a greater commitment from all people in every area of the company. **In the battle to defy mediocrity the domino effect can be one of your best weapons.**

Chapter 40. What is your style? It can make a huge difference!

"Men acquire a particular quality by constantly acting in a particular way."

Aristotle

There are two basic types of employees and managers. One is a proactive employee and the other is a reactive employee. There is, of course, a third type of employee or manager that I have seen all too frequently and that is the person who does nothing and hopes that the problem takes care of itself and goes away or that someone else will resolve the problem. These are most often procrastinators or people incapable of making a decision. You might call this type of employee the hemorrhoidal employee. They just sit on the problem and hope it goes away.

I know that this is not the type of employee or manager that you are, otherwise you would not be reading this book. Therefore, let's move back to our discussion about proactive and reactive employees and managers.

To simplify my writing, I will focus in on managers, but rest assured I am speaking of both managers and employees. I will use the term manager simply to avoid the redundancy of saying manager or employee repeatedly.

In my opinion, the majority of managers at all levels are reactive. The reactive manager manages, as the word indicates, by reacting to a situation or set of circumstances that has developed. Costs are high, so they react by trying to determine how to lower those costs. Returned products are increasing in number, so they look for ways to improve quality. Bills are late in going out, so they seek ways to speed up the billing process.

Past due accounts are paying even slower, so the reactive manager seeks out ways to speed up collections and get those past due bills in.

Absenteeism is high, so the reactive manager takes actions to stem this problem. Complaints are coming in more frequently, so the reactive manager takes steps to improve customer service.

"It is never very clever to solve problems. It is far cleverer not to have them."

E.F. Shumacher

In each and every case they have reacted to a problem. **This is the problem.** They have let the problem come into existence. They must now deal with the problem. Occasionally the reactive manager will act in a proactive manner, but this is much more infrequent.

The proactive manager is a manager who is often taken for granted. You see, the goal of the proactive manager is to think short and long term. He thinks today about tomorrow. His goal is to prevent problems from ever coming into existence. Of course, he must also manage as needed in a reactive style, usually addressing problems created by others, but, unlike the reactive manager, the proactive manager does this much less frequently since he has prevented so many problems from ever coming into existence.

The proactive manager is a rare and invaluable talent. Unfortunately, the very strengths of the proactive manager are what often leads him to be so unappreciated. By thinking short and long term, by planning ahead with foresight and decisiveness, the proactive manager never has to deal with many of the problems that the reactive manager must contend with.

The illusion, of course, is that the reactive manager is busier and therefore a more valuable manager. After all, look at all the problems he deals with every day. Look at all the fires he must put out. His desk is always a mess, covered with problems and projects. On the other hand, how important can the proactive manager be? He does not look that busy. His desk is normally clear and well organized. He does not put out fires and handle problems all day long. He is often taken for granted and under appreciated.

His department or division runs so much smoother than all the others it almost seems to run itself. Too good for his own good? Perhaps.

But which way would you rather have your company, division, or department run? Who would you rather work with or for?

By thinking both short and long term, the proactive manager improves every area he is responsible for. He thinks of yesterday, today, and tomorrow. He learns from yesterday's mistakes and missed opportunities to take steps to insure that they will not occur again in the future. When he must manage in a reactive manner he does so as quickly as possible considering the circumstances and does so in a decisive manner. He does not let the embers smolder. He puts the fire out.

He capitalizes on strengths while working to improve weaknesses in every area. He works to make sure it is done right the first time and, by doing so, does not have to worry about how to fix it or redo it when a problem comes up. By being proactive, he helps his company in numerous ways that are never seen. After all, you can see a correction to a problem but it is very difficult to see the problems that were prevented from ever occurring as a result of steps taken by the proactive manager weeks, months, or even years before.

An in-depth discussion of these styles will be the subject of another book but, in short, the proactive manager saves money, time, and frustration.

The exact same managerial philosophy used by the proactive manager will serve you best in your quest to pursue excellence and defy mediocrity. But it will be up to you to think in a preventive or proactive manner in conjunction with every area of operations that you are responsible for. It will be up to you to foster this style and attitude in others.

Control your quality at the beginning and you will have fewer rejects, reduced service demands, and an improved reputation for quality. This means lowers costs and higher selling prices. This means increased profits.

Hire right to begin with and you will have more loyal and productive employees. This means you will turn out better quality, lower cost work. This means less time hiring and training new employees. This means increased profits and better morale.

No matter what area of your business or department we are talking about, do it right the first time and you won't find yourself having to manage in a reactive style as often in the future. Think and act with an eye to both today and tomorrow.

If you take steps at the beginning to prevent problems or costs in the future, you will have no need to worry about the problem later on. <u>Let me give you a few more examples of what I am talking about, and, since taking a proactive approach is so important throughout the company let me use some examples of proactive corporate strategies.</u>

Taking the time to hire right will save the company personnel problems and costs. If they hire without taking the time to see enough people to enable them to hire the best person they can afford and if they hire without thoroughly checking out the person they are considering, it could be a very costly mistake.

Morale problems could result. Reduced productivity and / or quality could occur as a result of a poor hiring decision that could have been avoided. Increased sick time and workers' compensation costs could result if a person was hired with a poor or questionable history in these areas.

Higher unemployment costs could also result if the company was forced to, and was able to, correct the hiring mistake. This does not even consider the tremendous waste of time spent training an employee who did not work out and should not have been hired and the cost of hiring and training a new employee to replace this one. Nor does it consider the potential wrongful termination suit that could come in this suit happy society we live in.

Look at machinery. If someone purchases the lowest cost piece of equipment they can to resolve an immediate need, they are thinking only of the short term.

In the long term, however, consumable costs could be much higher than they would have been with a higher priced alternative product. The lower cost machine may break down more often and, since it has a poor warranty, the company could be paying higher service costs. Don't forget the lost time which lowers productivity and hinders the company's ability to service their customers.

By doing their homework they might have found out that the higher cost machine had a much better maintenance record and lower operating costs and, as a result, in the long run would have saved money, time, and frustration. They could have prevented numerous related problems by thinking about and analyzing both the short term and long term results of their actions and decisions.

What about lease rates for a facility? By properly negotiating a lease with an eye on both today and tomorrow the company could save significant amounts of money. A proactive manager would consider the rate today and build in controls to contain the rate each and every year of the lease. They would also include options for extensions as well as escape clauses. The proactive manager would dictate that all potential problem clauses are removed or negated. They do not want to deal with the cost or expense 5 years down the road.

I have a very high spirited Dalmatian named Niki. When I got Niki I took a proactive action by having my yard fenced in. Had I been reactive I might have found myself chasing her all over the neighborhood and might have even lost her. It is much easier to never let her out than it is to try and get her back home. I simply took steps to make sure I never have to deal with the problem.

Take a proactive attitude in everything you do. It will be much easier and less costly to prevent the problem from ever coming into existence.

Think of this as a form of preventive maintenance for every thing you do. Think. Plan ahead. Be proactive and not just reactive.

Chapter 41. Thinking. The ability that sets us apart from robots.

"Creativity can solve almost any problem. The creative act, the defeat of habit by originality, overcomes everything."

George Lois

We, you and I, are not robots. We can think. This ability is what sets us apart from robots. If we don't use this ability every day to do the best job we can, our employers are better off with robots. They never call in sick. They never take a break. They never take a vacation. They need no benefits. They will work 24 hours a day and never get paid a penny.

They can do all these things better than you and I. But they can't think. They can't question. They can't learn from their mistakes and improve. They can't engage in self-assessment. They do not have the greatest resource known to man. You have it.

You own it free and clear. Your mind is your greatest asset. To become the best you can become all you need to do is use it. To find a better way to do anything all you need to do is put that magnificent thinking machine to use.

We have the one thing capable of solving every problem we have. We have the key to our quest to be the best we can. The problem is we simply do not use it enough. We function too much as robots.

The late Earl Nightingale, much like Abraham Lincoln, would often use a short story to make his point. One of his stories comes to mind as an effective way to demonstrate the importance of asking questions and thinking creatively.

According to the story, many years ago when a person who owed money could be thrown into jail, a merchant in London had the misfortune to owe a huge sum of money to a mean moneylender. The moneylender, who was old and ugly, fancied the merchant's beautiful young daughter and he proposed a bargain.

He said he would cancel the merchant's debt if he could have the girl instead. Well, both the merchant and the daughter were horrified at this suggestion so the cunning money lender proposed that they let providence decide the matter. He told them that he would put a black pebble and a white pebble into an empty bag and that the girl would have to pick out one of the pebbles.

If she chose the black pebble, she would become his wife and her father's debt would be canceled. If she chose the white pebble, she would stay with her father and the debt would still be canceled. But if she refused to pick a pebble, her father would be thrown in jail and she would starve.

Well, reluctantly the merchant agreed. They were on a pebble strewn path in the merchants garden at the time as they talked. The moneylender stooped down to pick up the two pebbles. As he did, the girl, sharp-eyed with fright, noticed that he picked up two black pebbles and put them into the money bag. He wasn't taking any chances. He then asked the girl to decide her fate and that of her father.

Now I will interrupt this story to ask you, what would you have advised the girl to do?

The choices seem bleak. If you advise her to take a pebble to save her father she must sacrifice herself. If you advise her to refuse to take a pebble or to expose the moneylender as a cheat, her father goes to jail.

What would you advise her to do? Is there any way she can save both herself and her father? **If there was ever a time that showed the importance of creative thinking and innovation, this was certainly it.**

I will tell you what she did on the next page.

Well, the girl reached into the moneybag to pick a pebble. Without looking at it, she fumbled it and let it fall to the path where it became lost among all the others. "How clumsy of me," she said. "but don't worry, you'll be able to tell the color of the one I took by the color of the one remaining.".

Since the remaining pebble was, of course, black, it must be assumed that she had taken the white pebble. Since the moneylender could not dare to admit his dishonesty, the father's debt was forgiven and the girl remained with her father.

> *"Any activity becomes creative when the doer cares about doing it right, or better."*
>
> *John Updike*

Creative thinking, innovative approaches to problem solving, and the ability to adapt to ever-changing circumstances can be the sole reason a business survives. All too many think that these terms and functions apply only to areas like marketing, advertising, packaging, and new product development. **They are wrong.**

Creativity and innovation must be demonstrated throughout all levels of a company. These qualities should be fostered by management in employees.

These functions must be undertaken by someone within an organization, if that organization is to survive and grow.

<u>That someone should be you.</u> You must constantly be asking the questions and seeking the answers. You can make a difference. A big difference.

Chapter 42. You've got to have faith.

"I am looking for a lot of men who have an infinite capacity to not know what can't be done."

Henry Ford

You have got to have faith in yourself and your ability to do the job better. Think about how much faith those fine people that hired you had in you when they did hire you. They checked you out and made a decision to hire you based on many factors, but the most important factor was that they felt you could do the job and do it well.

These men and woman from human resources and management made a decision based on their faith in your ability to be a valuable asset to the company.

They took a chance with you. They took a chance that you would make them look good. Along with this came the chance you would make them look bad. If you did not work out, it would be a negative reflection on them that they made a bad decision in hiring you.

These people had faith in you and it is incumbent on you to live up to the expectations they had when they hired you. Don't ever doubt you can do the job and do it very well. The people who hired you are professionals. In their opinion you can do the job. Strive to prove them right, to justify their faith in you.

"Impossible is a word to be found only in the dictionary of fools."

Napoleon Bonaparte

Have faith in your own abilities and in the abilities of others to recognize and reward your abilities and efforts. It starts with you. It always does. How you think about your capabilities is most important.

Mediocrity loves self-doubt and low self-esteem. Defy it.

"Whether you think you can or think you can't, you are right."

Henry Ford

Most of us are far more capable than we allows ourselves to think we are. We all have a tendency to think of why we can't succeed. Of why we will fail. Of why something won't work. We fear failure. We worry about the ridicule of others.

We see the obstacles and not the opportunities. We hold ourselves back. We allow self-doubt to replace self-confidence. We tell ourselves why we can't and shouldn't and by doing so justify not even trying. This causes us to fail without even giving ourselves the opportunity to succeed.

We are most often our own worst enemy. We hold ourselves back. We prevent ourselves from improving and pursuing excellence.

<u>Have a little faith in yourself. After all, you don't want to let those down who hired you do you? As importantly, you don't want to let yourself down.</u>

Chapter 43. Go looking for responsibility.

"Do the thing and you shall have the power."

Emerson

Most people don't want responsibility. They don't want the pressure of having to make decisions and of having responsibility for results. They may say they do and they may want the money or promotion, but the reality is that they don't want responsibility.

They will hide from responsibility and avoid decisions or, at best, make a decision based on the way the corporate wind may be blowing.

Yes, most people will run from responsibility faster than a cat will run from a dog.

A person in search of added responsibility will not have to look very far. Much like mediocrity surrounds you, the opportunity to gain added responsibility presents itself at every turn.

Whenever you see the chance to extend yourself, take it. Whenever you see a chance to do more than that which is expected of you, do it. Whenever you see someone you can help, help them. When you see a deed that others are ignoring, do it.

Don't wait for someone to come to you and give you responsibility. Take it and prove you can handle it and you will have it.

Taking responsibility will make you more valuable and important. Others will support you and look up to you or look out for you. Both very desirable benefits.

Don't wait for someone else to decide to give it to you. Look for it, take it, and start controlling your own future.

Defy Mediocrity: <u>The</u> Employee's 90 Minute Guide To Excellence

Chapter 44. "I don't know."

"There is no disgrace in not knowing when knowledge does not rest with you; the disgrace is in being unwilling to learn."

Benedetto Varchi

"I don't know.". For many, these words are terrifying. A big problem is that many are afraid to admit this. Instead, they make assumptions, avoid action, are unable to make a decision or make an uninformed decision.

I have seen countless numbers of people who have failed or, at the very least, stalled, in their careers because they were afraid to ask questions and admit they did not know something or needed help. Somehow they felt this made them look stupid, or less than effective, or less than perfect, or inadequate.

But there is nothing wrong with saying "I don't know.". There is nothing wrong with not knowing or understanding something.

I will never understand this fragility of ego. Isn't it true that we all know nothing until we are taught? Isn't it true that we often need to be told the same things over and over? Do you not remember watching a child learn to walk? Isn't it true they fall down over and over again until they start taking one step, then two steps, and three before they are walking?

No, there is nothing wrong with admitting you do not know something or do not understand something. Quite the opposite, in fact. However, there is something wrong with not finding out what you need to know. There is something terribly wrong with making assumptions instead of asking for assistance.

The employee in pursuit of improvement, in pursuit of excellence, puts his ego aside and defies mediocrity by seeking the needed clarification, the needed information. They are not afraid to say "I don't know" or "I don't understand.

Derrick W. Welch

Chapter 45. Relentless.

"There's no future in saying it can't be done."

Harvey Mackay

You must be relentless in your pursuit of improvement. In what you do and how you do it. In how you service your customer, internal and external. In how you perform.

It is not a one shot deal. It is not something you can work at when you think about it or have time. It is not something you can spend a few weeks working on and consider it done.

The pursuit of excellence does not have a finish line. You will never reach the point where no further improvement is possible. Improvement is always possible. You will never be able to say "I can't become better.".

If you are to defy mediocrity, you must work at it every day. You must do the best job you can while constantly thinking of how you can do a better job and how you can make the company better.

Mediocrity is a powerful adversary. It has many allies. It surrounds you. To defeat it, to rise above it, you must be relentless in your efforts to do what you do better. Not just for a few days or weeks. Not just before your annual review is coming up. Not just when you think someone is paying attention to what you are doing.

To do the best job you can and to become better at what you do, you must be relentless.

Chapter 46. Versatility.

"Always do more than is required of you."

George S. Patton

You should cross train yourself in as many other areas of the company's operation as you can. This will accomplish a number of things. It will give you more knowledge about your company and customers. Increased knowledge in these areas will allow you to ask more questions and find more ways to improve. The more you know about how and why things are done, the more opportunity you have to improve the way things are done.

Cross training also enables you to become more skilled and, therefore, a more valuable employee. It demonstrates initiative and commitment.

It will give you a greater understanding and appreciation of job responsibilities between departments and of what other people really do and how they do it. This will allow you to see how each person and department interacts and how they depend on your efforts and the efforts of others.

This will give your internal customer service efforts a tremendous boost. The more you can improve internal customer service, the more you will improve productivity, quality, and external customer service. All of which result in lower costs and higher profits.

It will make you more valuable, as you will now be able to step in and help others when they are busy and you are slow. This will also provide variety to you while serving to give you an inside view of the other departments within the company you may one day wish to work in on a primary basis.

Every team places great value on versatility.

Chapter 47.   It is your company.

"To defy mediocrity merely do your job as though you yourself owned the company."

Derrick W. Welch

"I am not management." "It's not my company." "I only work here." The mind-set of mediocrity.

The mind-set of excellence says "It is my company." It is my job." "It is my responsibility.".

Start thinking and start acting as though the company was yours and you will start seeing changes in your attitude and effort that you can't even imagine.

It is a powerful change in mind-set. Things you never even used to think about will begin to interest you. Things you never even considered will begin to bother you. Your commitment will dramatically improve. You will constantly think of how you can do better and become better.

Ideas for individual improvement, as well as corporate improvement, will suddenly appear in your mind. You will do more for your career than just about anything else you could ever do.

You do not have to be a manager or supervisor to have responsibility. You do not have to be an owner or an executive to put the company's interests first. **Do your job as though you yourself owned the company and maybe one day you will.**

Never forget that unless the company survives you will not have a job. Unless the company prospers it will be unable to help you accomplish your goals.

From reporting theft to answering a ringing phone, from shutting off the lights to keeping your working area safe and clean, you have a responsibility.

A responsibility to do the best you can. A responsibility to look out for the company's interests as though it was your own. Acceptance of this responsibility is one more example of how you can defy mediocrity.

The employee who refuses to answer a phone ringing off the hook is embracing mediocrity. The employee who lets mistakes slide because they are "not responsible" is demonstrating mediocrity. An employee who could do better but doesn't does not deserve to even keep the job he has never mind advance within the organization.

The voice of mediocrity says "It is not my job.". The voice of excellence says "It is my job. It is my company.".

Chapter 48. Your battle plan to defeat mediocrity.

"Most successful men have not achieved their distinction by having some new talent or opportunity presented to them. They have developed the opportunity that was at hand."

Bruce Barton

Mediocrity surrounds you. As an employer, employee, or customer you are face to face with it every day. Every time you deal with someone who could do their job better, much better in most cases, you are dealing with a creature of mediocrity.

Every time you could do your job better and don't, you become a creature of mediocrity.

So many in the ranks of mediocrity and so few in the ranks of excellence. Which do you choose do be in? I have given you many tools you can use in your pursuit of excellence. Here are a few more.

♦ Always try to help others. The day may come when they help you, including possibly saving your job or supporting your promotion. But don't do it for these reasons. Do it because it is the right thing to do. The benefits will follow one day.

♦ Tackle the jobs no one else wants.

♦ Always try to exceed expectations. Do more than you are asked to do and that you are expected to do. Extend yourself.

"It is far more important to be able to hit the target than it is to haggle over who makes a weapon or pulls the trigger."

◆ <u>Stop worrying about who gets the credit or who gets the blame and worry instead about getting the job done.</u> Don't step up and try to grab the credit. Rarely will one person deserve all the credit or, for that matter, all the blame. Others will always resent someone who tries to grab the credit and assign the blame.

Don't you resent this when others do it? Share the credit and the blame. You will succeed with the help of others and fail without it.

◆ <u>Make sure you are fully aware of what your company's objectives are and how you and those in your department fit in.</u> What are the objectives? Improved quality? Increased sales? Higher profits? More rapid service? The point is to understand the larger objectives and what role you play in reaching them.

There is a big picture involved. Think of the big picture as a puzzle. You are a piece of that puzzle. No matter how small or insignificant you might think your job is remember, the puzzle will never be completed properly without your part or piece.

Also remember, no matter how large you think your piece in the overall puzzle is, it will never be completed without all the other small pieces. Never overestimate or underestimate your importance.

◆ <u>Enthusiasm.</u> Everyone likes to work with those who are enthusiastic. They are more enjoyable to work with and to work for. They make work more enjoyable. Be enthusiastic. It is contagious.

If you are like most people, you enjoy working with enthusiastic co-workers much more than with sour puss whiners. Don't you think your co-workers and bosses feel the same way?

◆ <u>Dependability.</u> People must be able to count on you to be at the job, to do it as well as you can, and to do what you promise you will do. No matter how talented you may be, unless you are on the job you are of no value to the company or your co-workers.

◆ <u>A commitment to working hard.</u> Remember, all companies want to increase profits. This is the objective of being in business. To accomplish this they need many things. One of these is people who are not afraid of hard work.

"It is O.K. to disagree as long as you are not disagreeable."

Bill Walton

◆ <u>An ability to get along with others.</u> The work force is made up of a wide variety of people. It would be naive to think you will have good chemistry with all of them or that you will like and respect all of them.

Nor will all of them like and respect you. If they did it would be an ideal world, but despite what some motivational speakers and authors might tell you, this simply is not going to happen.

But this does not matter. This is not the objective. The objective is to be able to get along with your co-workers in a manner that maximizes your results and their results.

◆ <u>Resourcefulness.</u> Being resourceful is a valued quality in any business. Being able to think of better ways to do things. Being able to identify and solve problems. Being able to help others improve the results they produce. Asking the questions and finding the answers.

◆ <u>Do every job as though your job depended on it.</u> It might!

"Assumption must never replace effort."

Derrick W. Welch

◆ <u>If in doubt ask.</u>

If you do not fully understand something, ask for clarification! Never assume, always ask.

"The secret of joy in work is contained in one word-- excellence. To know how to do something well is to enjoy it."

Pearl Buck

When you do the best job you can, you will enjoy your job much more. The pride you take in your abilities and accomplishments will carry over into all areas of your life. There is no question about this. You can't just turn mediocrity on and off. You can't do an average job at work and then pursue excellence off the job.

Mediocrity is an insidious enemy. It will dog you in every area of your life. You must defy it on the job to defeat it.

"The seeds of dissatisfaction will produce a harvest of change."

Derrick W. Welch

The key to success in any type of improvement plan is that the attitude of acceptance for the old way of doing things must be replaced by an attitude of doing things a new and better way. Commitment must replace complacency. Action must replace apathy.

It begins with you.

If you follow the guidelines I have given you in this book, you will be maximizing your talents, capabilities, and career opportunities. But I can only give you the tools.

You must wield them. You must take the initiative. You must make the commitment. You must analyze your weakness and determine how to improve yourself and your capabilities and then take the needed steps to do it.

"Choose to be uncommon. Think of the alternative."

Derrick W. Welch

I know it is hard to believe that the simple traits I have given you in this book would place you in the minority of employees. But I assure you they will.

Mediocrity is an enemy in your mind. The easiest of all enemies to defy. The rewards of victory will astound you.

There is only one person who can stop you from becoming the best you can at what you do. The person in the mirror.

I won't wish you luck because if you follow the advice in this book you won't need it.

My best,

Derrick W. Welch

Defy Mediocrity: The Employee's 90 Minute Guide To Excellence

About the author.

Derrick Welch is currently Chief Operating Officer and Vice President of a multi-million dollar Massachusetts based company that manufactures and distributes products for sale nationwide. Prior to that he served as Vice President of Client Services for a major Boston-based advertising agency for 6 years. Mr. Welch has degrees in business administration, marketing, and management.

Derrick has a simple goal. It is to help you succeed. It is to help you reach your professional goals. He hopes this book is a strong start in that direction. Derrick can be contacted through our offices.

Derrick is also the author of our best-selling title "In Pursuit of Profits: How To At Least Double Your Profits Without Increasing Your Sales". This book includes over 1,000 cost control, expense reduction, and income producing strategies. To order this book please see the order form at the end of this book.

If you would like to be placed on our mailing list please write us at:

> **LeeMar Publishing**
> **Suite 178**
> **319 Centre Ave**
> **Rockland, MA 02370**

Your comments and suggestions regarding this book are both welcome and appreciated!

Derrick W. Welch

Additional copies of "Defy Mediocrity: <u>The</u> Employee's 90 Minute Guide To Excellence" can be ordered from LeeMar Publishing by phone, fax, or mail.

Single copies   **$10.95 each**

<u>**Discounts are available for multiple copy purchases. Please call for pricing based on the quantity you need.**</u>

To insure prompt and safe delivery all orders are shipped via UPS unless otherwise requested.

<u>Individual orders</u> must be prepaid and must include $4 shipping and handling for the first book and $.50 for each additional book. Individual orders from residents of MA please include 5% sales tax.

<u>Corporate orders</u> from publicly held companies need only indicate a purchase order number. Shipping, FOB Rockland, MA will be added to your invoice. MA orders will also incur a 5% added sales tax.

Ship to: Name _____

Title _____

Company_____

Address_____

City_____State _____Zip_____

Purchase Order #_____ Phone # _____

LeeMar Publishing

319 Centre Ave., Suite 178, Rockland, MA 02370
Phone 1-617-499-1970◆Fax 1-617-871-6025

Thank you for your order!

In Pursuit Of Profits

Few things will have a more positive impact on your career than efforts and ideas that directly impact your employer's bottom line.

Whether you are an executive, manager, or employee, **"In Pursuit of Profits: How To At Least Double Your Profits Without Increasing Your Sales"** by Derrick W. Welch can show you how to add tremendous value to your employer's bottom line and, by doing so, increase your impact with your company.

In fact, because so many, from virtually every type of industry, have realized the tremendous impact the strategies and concepts outlined in this book can have on the bottom line of their company and careers, **"In Pursuit of Profits: How To At Least Double Your Profits Without Increasing Your Sales"** has, by far and away, become our best-selling title.

This book will show you:

- *That the real objective is to produce profits, not products or services.*
- *The 5% solution. The secret to doubling profits without increasing sales.*
- *How to turn the sales force from order takers into salespeople.*
- *How your actions or inactions have far reaching effects on the bottom line.*
- *How to dramatically improve cash flow in all areas.*
- *How to get other employees enthusiastic about cutting costs and controlling expenses.*
- *Why business can be pretty complex, but why making more money is quite simple.*
- *The keys to total cost control.*
- *The difference between a proactive and a reactive management style.*
- *Why objectives without actionable goals are nothing more than dreams.*
- *How small savings result in big increases to the bottom line.*
- *The vital importance of the example you demonstrate.*
- *How to double your profits by controlling the purchasing process.*
- *How to slash overnight mail and shipping costs by 40% or more.*
- *How to slash the cost of owning company cars.*
- *How to increase credit availability while decreasing borrowing-related costs.*
- *Why customer service is one of your best marketing tools.*
- *How to eliminate credit risks while dramatically lowering credit and collection costs.*
- *How to cut the costs of buying and maintaining any type of equipment 25% to 50%.*
- *How to reduce facility-related costs by 25% or more.*
- *How to dramatically improve the cost effectiveness of your marketing programs.*
- *How to reduce personnel costs while increasing productivity.*
- *How to reduce phone and fax related expenses by 25% to 50%.*
- *Why controlling expenses and cutting costs have far more impact on the bottom line than increasing sales.*
- *How to cut costs in every area of the company to the bone without any sacrifice in quality or service.*

These are just some of the areas covered in this one-of-a-kind book. Unlike most business books on the market today this book contains no theory, no academic nonsense, no idealistic processes.

What it contains is over 1,000 down to earth, hard-hitting, actionable strategies that you can start using immediately to dramatically impact your company's daily cash flow and bottom line.

In fact, as the Chief Operating Officer of a multi-million dollar distributor / manufacturer Mr. Welch used these same strategies to increase this company's profits by 450% in the first two years after he took over operations.

If you are an employee, the strategies contained in this book can help provide you with the edge you need to move ahead in your career. Few things will have a more positive impact on your career than things you do that have a positive impact on your employer's bottom line.

If you are a business owner or division head, putting a copy of this book in the hands of each of your employees, or at least in the hands of your managers, will make a dramatic difference in the profitability of your company.

Based on the feedback we have received from executives and employees of companies around the country, large and small, including dozens of Fortune 500 companies, who have purchased copies of "In Pursuit of Profits" we feel confident in stating that should you decide to purchase "In Pursuit of Profits" it will be one of the best investments you could ever make.

To order your copy today please use the order form on the next page.

**Copies of "In Pursuit of Profits: How To At Least Double
Your Profits Without Increasing Your Sales" can be ordered
from LeeMar Publishing by phone, fax, or mail.**

Single copies $34.95 each

**Discounts are available for multiple copy purchases. Please call for pricing
based on the quantity you need.**

To insure prompt and safe delivery all orders are shipped via UPS unless
otherwise requested.

Individual orders must be prepaid and must include $5 shipping and handling
for the first book and $1 for each additional book. Individual orders from
residents of MA must include 5% sales tax.

Corporate orders from publicly held companies need only indicate a purchase
order number. Shipping, FOB Rockland, MA will be added to your invoice.
MA orders will also incur a 5% added sales tax.

Ship to: Name _____

Title _____

Company_____

Address_____

City_____State _____Zip_____

Purchase Order #_____ **Phone #** _____

LeeMar Publishing

319 Centre Ave., Suite 178, Rockland, MA 02370
Phone 1-617-499-1970◆Fax 1-617-871-6025

Thank you for your order!